HOW TO
MAKE A
NEW YORK
WILL

Third Edition

James L. Rogers

Mark Warda
Attorneys at Law

SPHINX® PUBLISHING
AN IMPRINT OF SOURCEBOOKS, INC.®
NAPERVILLE, ILLINOIS
www.SphinxLegal.com

Third Edition, 2004

Published by: **Sphinx® Publishing, An Imprint of Sourcebooks, Inc.®**

Naperville Office
P.O. Box 4410
Naperville, Illinois 60567-4410
630-961-3900
Fax: 630-961-2168
www.sourcebooks.com
www.SphinxLegal.com

This publication is designed to provide accurate and authoritative information in regard to the subject matter covered. It is sold with the understanding that the publisher is not engaged in rendering legal, accounting, or other professional service. If legal advice or other expert assistance is required, the services of a competent professional person should be sought.

From a Declaration of Principles Jointly Adopted by a Committee of the
American Bar Association and a Committee of Publishers and Associations

This product is not a substitute for legal advice.

Disclaimer required by Texas statutes.

Library of Congress Cataloging-in-Publication Data
Rogers, James L., 1965-
   How to make a New York will / by James L. Rogers and Mark Warda.-- 3rd
ed.
      p. cm.
   Includes index.
   ISBN 1-57248-401-2 (alk. paper)
   1. Wills--New York (State)--Popular works. I. Warda, Mark. II. Title.

KFN5201.Z9 R64 2004
346.74705'4--dc22
                                             2004024494

Printed and bound in the United States of America.
VHG Paperback — 10 9 8 7 6 5 4 3 2 1

CONTENTS

Using Self-Help Law Books

Before using a self-help law book, you should realize the advantages and disadvantages of doing your own legal work and understand the challenges and diligence that this requires.

The Growing Trend

Rest assured that you won't be the first or only person handling your own legal matter. For example, in some states, more than seventy-five percent of the people in divorces and other cases represent themselves. Because of the high cost of legal services, this is a major trend and many courts are struggling to make it easier for people to represent themselves. However, some courts are not happy with people who do not use attorneys and refuse to help them in any way. For some, the attitude is, "Go to the law library and figure it out for yourself."

We write and publish self-help law books to give people an alternative to the often complicated and confusing legal books found in most law libraries. We have made the explanations of the law as simple and easy to understand as possible. Of course, unlike an attorney advising an individual client, we cannot cover every conceivable possibility.

Cost Value Analysis

Whenever you shop for a product or service, you are faced with various levels of quality and price. In deciding what product or service to buy, you make a cost/value analysis on the basis of your willingness to pay and the quality you desire.

When buying a car, you decide whether you want transportation, comfort, status, or sex appeal. Accordingly, you decide among such choices as a Neon, a Lincoln, a Rolls Royce, or a Porsche. Before making a decision, you usually weigh the merits of each option against the cost.

When you get a headache, you can take a pain reliever (such as aspirin) or visit a medical specialist for a neurological examination. Given this choice, most people, of course, take a pain reliever, since it costs only pennies; whereas a medical examination costs hundreds of dollars and takes a lot of time. This is usually a logical choice because it is rare to need anything more than a pain reliever for a headache. But in some cases, a headache may indicate a brain tumor and failing to see a specialist right away can result in complications. Should everyone with a headache go to a specialist? Of course not, but people treating their own illnesses must realize that they are betting on the basis of their cost/value analysis of the situation. They are taking the most logical option.

The same cost/value analysis must be made when deciding to do one's own legal work. Many legal situations are very straight forward, requiring a simple form and no complicated analysis. Anyone with a little intelligence and a book of instructions can handle the matter without outside help.

But there is always the chance that complications are involved that only an attorney would notice. To simplify the law into a book like this, several legal cases often must be condensed into a single sentence or paragraph. Otherwise, the book would be several hundred pages long and too complicated for most people. However, this simplification necessarily leaves out many details and nuances that would apply to special or unusual situations. Also, there are many ways to interpret most legal questions. Your case may come before a judge who disagrees with the analysis of our authors.

Therefore, in deciding to use a self-help law book and to do your own legal work, you must realize that you are making a cost/value analysis. You have decided that the money you will save in doing it yourself outweighs the chance that your case will not turn out to your satisfaction. Most people handling their own simple legal matters never have a problem, but occasionally people find that it ended up costing them more to have an attorney straighten out the situation than it would have if they had hired an attorney in the beginning. Keep this in mind while handling your case, and be sure to consult an attorney if you feel you might need further guidance.

Local Rules The next thing to remember is that a book which covers the law for the entire nation, or even for an entire state, cannot possibly include every procedural difference of every jurisdiction. Whenever possible, we provide the exact form needed; however, in some areas, each county, or even each judge, may require unique forms and procedures. In our state books, our forms usually cover the majority of counties in the state, or provide examples of the type of form which will be required. In our national books, our forms are sometimes even more general in nature but are designed to give a good idea of the type of form that will be needed in most locations. Nonetheless, keep in mind that your state, county, or judge may have a requirement, or use a form, that is not included in this book.

You should not necessarily expect to be able to get all of the information and resources you need solely from within the pages of this book. This book will serve as your guide, giving you specific information whenever possible and helping you to find out what else you will need to know. This is just like if you decided to build your own backyard deck. You might purchase a book on how to build decks. However, such a book would not include the building codes and permit requirements of every city, town, county, and township in the nation; nor would it include the lumber, nails, saws, hammers, and other materials and tools you would need to actually build the deck. You would use the book as your guide, and then do some work and research involving such matters as whether you need a permit of some kind, what type and grade of wood are available in your area, whether to use hand tools or power tools, and how to use those tools.

Before using the forms in a book like this, you should check with your court clerk to see if there are any local rules of which you should be aware, or local forms you will need to use. Often, such forms will require the same information as the forms in the book but are merely laid out differently or use slightly different language. They will sometimes require additional information.

Changes in the Law Besides being subject to local rules and practices, the law is subject to change at any time. The courts and the legislatures of all fifty states are constantly revising the laws. It is possible that while you are reading this book, some aspect of the law is being changed.

In most cases, the change will be of minimal significance. A form will be redesigned, additional information will be required, or a waiting period will be extended. As a result, you might need to revise a form, file an extra form, or wait out a longer time period; these types of changes will not usually affect the outcome of your case. On the other hand, sometimes a major part of the law is changed, the entire law in a particular area is rewritten, or a case that was the basis of a central legal point is overruled. In such instances, your entire ability to pursue your case may be impaired.

Again, you should weigh the value of your case against the cost of an attorney and make a decision as to what you believe is in your best interest.

Introduction

This book's intent is to give New York residents a basic understanding of the laws regarding wills, joint property, and other types of ownership of property as they affect their estate planning. It is designed to allow those with simple estates to set up their affairs quickly and inexpensively and to distribute their property according to their wishes.

It also includes information on appointing a guardian for minor children. This can be useful in avoiding bad feelings between relatives and in protecting the children from being raised by someone to whom you would object.

Chapters 1 through 5 explain the laws which control wills. Chapters 6 and 7 discuss living wills, powers of attorney, and anatomical gifts. Appendix A contains sample filled-in will forms. Appendix B contains blank will forms you can tear out or photocopy.

You can prepare your own will quickly and easily by using the forms out of the book or by photocopying them. You can retype the material on blank paper if you prefer. The small amount of time it takes to do this can give you and your heirs the peace of mind of knowing that your estate will be distributed according to your wishes.

A surprising number of people have had their estates pass to the wrong parties because of a simple lack of knowledge. Before using any of the forms in Appendix B, you should read and understand the material in this book.

If your situation is at all complicated you are advised to seek the advice of an attorney. In many communities, wills are available for very reasonable prices. No book of this type can cover every contingency in every case, but a knowledge of the basics will help you make the right decisions regarding your property.

I | BASIC RULES YOU SHOULD KNOW

What is a Will?

A *will* is a document you can use to control who gets your property, who will be guardian of your children, and who will manage your estate.

Using a Will

Some people think a will avoids *probate*. It does not. A will is the document used in probate to determine who receives your property. It also appoints guardians and personal representatives.

Note: *Probate is the court procedure for settling a person's affairs after they have died. Through probate, a person's (the decendant's) property is passed or transferred to creditors and/or beneficiaries pursuant to the decendant's wishes or by operation of law.*

If you wish to avoid probate you need to use methods other than a will, such as joint ownership, pay-on-death accounts, or living trusts. However, everyone should have a will in case some property, which was forgotten or received just prior to death, does not avoid probate for some reason.

Spouse's Elective Share

Under New York law, a *surviving spouse* may have the right not to accept the property they are given under your will but rather take what is called an *elective share*. This share is one-third of your net estate if you are survived by one or more *issue* or descendants (children, grandchildren, etc.) and one-half of your net estate if there are no descendants alive at the time of your death. This is the case no matter what your will states. Moreover, you can not avoid this rule by giving away your property during your life in the form of *joint tenancies, revocable trusts,* or gifts made in contemplation of your death. New York has cleverly prevented people from making such lifetime transfers to defeat a spouse's right to elect against a will by calling them *testamentary substitutes* and by including their value in your estate.

The only real way that you can defeat your spouse's right of election is if your spouse *releases* this right as in a *prenuptial* or *postnuptial agreement*. So if your desire is that your spouse not be able to claim the elective share, you should have a properly drawn agreement stating that your spouse releases this statutory right.

Community Property Issues

New York is not a *community property state*. This means that New York does not have laws that treat property that you and your spouse acquire during your marriage as community property. If New York were to treat all your property acquired during marriage as community property, your spouse would be considered as a one-half owner of all such property.

While New York is not a community property state, New York does look at all personal property that you may have once acquired with your spouse in a community property state as community property. Therefore, if you once lived in a community property state (Arizona, California, Idaho, Nevada, New Mexico, Texas, Washington, or Wisconsin), all personal property acquired by you and your spouse in that community property state will continue to remain as community property after you move to New York. The end result is that upon your death, your spouse will be entitled to one-half of that community property. So if you have lived in other states before moving to New York, you should keep a record of which property was acquired before or after your move.

Joint Tenancy

Where a will gives property to one person but it is already in a *joint account* with another person, the will is ignored and the joint owner of the account gets the property. This is because the property in the account *avoids* probate and *passes directly* to the joint owner. A will only controls property that goes through probate.

There are exceptions to this rule. If some money is put into a joint account only for convenience, it might pass under the will. However, if the joint owner does not give it up, it could take an expensive court battle to get it back.

Example 1: Bill's will leaves all his property to his friend, Mary. Bill dies owning only a house jointly with his sister, Joan, and a bank account jointly with his son, Don. Joan gets the house. Don gets the bank account. His friend, Mary, gets nothing.

Example 2: Betty's will leaves half her assets to Ann and half her assets to George. Betty dies owning $1,000,000 in stock jointly with George and a car in her own name. Ann gets only a half interest in the car. George gets all the stock and half the car.

Example 3: John's will leaves all his property equally to his five children. Before going in the hospital ,he names his oldest son, Harry, as joint owner of his accounts. John does this because he wants to make sure that Harry can take money out of his accounts to pay John's bills. John dies and Harry gets all of John's accounts amounting to $150,000, which is the only property that John leaves. John could have avoided this problem if he had given Harry a power of attorney (discussed in Chapter 6) to manage John's property, rather than naming Harry as a joint account owner.

In each of these cases the property went to a person it probably should not have because the decedent did not realize that joint ownership overruled their will. In some families, this might not be a problem. From the third example, Harry might divide up the property equally (and possibly pay a gift tax.) But in many cases, Harry would just keep everything and the family would never talk to him again.

Avoiding Probate

While the above cases show how joint tenancy can defeat a person's estate plan, if used properly, joint tenancy can help avoid probate and simplify your estate.

Example 1: When Ed and Suzanne married they put all their property and bank accounts in joint tenancy. When either of them dies, the other will inherit all property without a probate.

Example 2: Ethel's only heir is her forty-year-old granddaughter. She lives in a retirement home and her only assets are her bank CDs. She names her granddaughter as joint owner on the CDs. When she dies, the granddaughter may go to the bank and cash them without a probate procedure.

Risk

The above cases may make it appear that joint tenancy is the answer to all problems, but it often creates *more* problems. If you put your real estate in joint ownership with someone, you cannot sell it or mortgage it without that person's signature. If you put your bank account in joint ownership with someone, they can take out all of your money at any time, including before you die.

Example 1: In the first example above, if Ed had a lot of property and Suzanne had none when they married, putting it in joint tenancy may make it look like a gift to the court if there were a divorce. If Ed kept it all in his own name, he might not lose it in a divorce.

Example 2: Alice put her house in joint ownership with her son. She later married Joe and moved in with him. She wanted to sell her house and to invest the money for income. Her son refused to sign the deed. She would be forced to go to court for an order making her son sign a deed, which would be expensive and possibly unsuccessful.

Example 3: Alex put his bank accounts into joint ownership with his daughter Mary to avoid probate. Mary fell in love with Doug who was

✪ other money or personal property up to the value of $15,000.

You cannot avoid this exemption from your estate with any provision in your will. The only way that it can be avoided, with respect to your spouse, is if your spouse relinquishes this right such as in a *premarital agreement* or a *postmarital agreement.* Moreover, any such relinquishment must specifically mention that your spouse is relinquishing all rights to claim the exemption.

Example: Donna died leaving an automobile that she owned in tenancy in common with her surviving husband. Donna's executor claimed that the surviving husband could not claim Donna's one-half ownership interest of $6,000 in the car because even if it were considered exempt property, Donna's husband had executed a prenuptial agreement relinquishing all statutory interests in his wife's estate. The court disagreed, holding that Donna's ownership interest was exempt property and that since the prenuptial agreement did not specifically mention that Donna's husband had waived his right to claim the exemption, the husband did not relinquish his right. The result was that Donna's husband was entitled to Donna's one-half ownership interest of $6,000 as exempt property.

Getting Married after Making Your Will

If you get married after making your will and do not rewrite it after the wedding, your spouse gets a share of your estate as if you had no will unless you have a prenuptial agreement, you made a provision for your spouse in the will, or you stated in the will that you intended not to mention your prospective spouse.

Example: John made out his will leaving everything to his disabled brother. When he married Joan, an heiress with plenty of money, he didn't change his will because he still wanted his brother to get his estate. When he died, Joan got his entire estate and his brother got nothing.

Children Born after Making Your Will

If you make a will and do not mention a child who is born after you sign that will, that child will nevertheless be considered a beneficiary of your will in New York. The share of your estate taken by the child born after you sign your will depends on whether you have provided for any other child in your will. If you have provided for a child or children in your will, the child born after you make your will is entitled to an equal share of all of the property that you have given to your child or children named in your will. If you have not named any child or children as beneficiaries in your will, then your child born after you make your will is entitled to his or her intestate share (the share such child would have received if you died without making a will).

The goal of this rule of law is to ensure that children born after a will is signed are not prevented from sharing in your estate simply because you may have forgotten to add them to your will. So if you desire that no children born after you sign your will become a part of your will, you should consider adding a clause in your will that specifically states this.

Debts

One of the duties of the person administering an estate is to pay the *debts* of the decedent. Before an estate is distributed, the legitimate debts must be ascertained and paid.

An exception is *secured debts*. These are debts that are protected by a lien against property, like a home loan or a car loan. In the case of a secured debt, the loan does not have to be paid before the property is distributed.

Example: John owns a $100,000 house with a $80,000 mortgage and he has $100,000 in the bank. If he leaves the house to his brother and the bank account to his sister, then his brother would get the home but would owe the $80,000 mortgage.

People cannot inherit another's debts. A person's property is used to pay their probate and funeral expenses first. If there is not enough to pay his or her debts, then the creditors are out of luck. However, if a person leaves property to people and does not have enough assets to pay his or her debts then the property will be sold to pay the debts.

Example: Jeb's will leaves all of his property to his three children. At the time of his death Jeb has $30,000 in medical bills, $11,000 in credit card debt, and his only assets are his car and $5,000 in stock. The car and stock would be sold and the funeral bill and probate fees paid out of the proceeds. If any money was left it would go to the creditors and nothing would be left for the children. The children would not have to pay the medical bills or credit card debt.

Estate and Inheritance Taxes

There is a federal estate tax for estates above a certain amount. Estates below that amount are allowed a *unified credit* that exempts them from tax. The unified credit applies to the estate a person can leave at death and to gifts during his or her lifetime. In 2004, the amount exempted by the unified credit is $1,500,000, but it will rise to $2,000,000 by the year 2006 and 3,500,000 by year 2009. In 2010 the credit is scheduled to be unlimited (which means that no estate will be subject to an estate tax), but it is scheduled to return to 1,000,000 after 2010. The amount will change according to the following schedule.

Year	Amount
2004-2005	$1,500,000
2006-2008	$2,000,000
2009	$3,500,000
2010	Repealed
2011	$1,000,000

There is also a New York state tax for estates above $1,000,000. (This amount, unlike the federal credit above, is not scheduled to increase at the time this book was published.) The New York state estate tax only applies to those persons who die as a resident of New York state. Decendents who are not residents of New York are also subject to this estate tax with respect to their real or personal property having an actual situs in New York.

Annual Exclusion

When a person makes a gift, that gift is subtracted from the amount entitled to the unified credit available to his or her estate at death. However, a person is allowed to make gifts of up to $11,000 per person per year without having these subtracted from the unified credit. This means a married couple can make gifts of up to $20,000 per person.

> **Example:** In 2004, Tina makes a $20,000 gift to her son, Tom. Tina would need to file a gift tax return for 2004. The first $11,000 of the gift would not use up any of her $1,500,000 federal unified credit. However the excess of the gift beyond the $11,000 would reduce her credit (i.e., it would reduce her credit by $9,000).

Unlimited Marital Deduction

If you are married, you can transfer an unlimited amount of your property both during your lifetime and upon your death to your spouse without worrying about any gift or estate tax. This special rule is called the *marital deduction.*

2 NEEDING A NEW YORK WILL

A will allows you to decide who gets your property after your death. You can give specific personal items to certain persons and decide which of your friends or relatives deserve a greater share of your estate. You can also leave gifts to schools and charities.

A will allows you to decide who will be the *executor* (male) or *executrix* (female) of your estate. An executor or executrix is the person who gathers all your assets and distributes them to the beneficiaries. A will also allows you to choose a *guardian* for your minor children. This way you can avoid fights among relatives and make sure the best person raises your children.

Distributions with No Will

If you do not have a New York will, New York law says that your property must be distributed as follows.

- ✪ If you are survived by a spouse and issue, $50,000 and one-half of the value of your estate beyond that amount will go to your spouse. Anything left over after your spouse's share is distributed goes to your issue by representation.

(The term *issue* is defined as your descendants in any degree. Thus issue would include your children and grandchildren. The term *by representation* means that any of your estate allocated to your issue will be allocated in equal shares to your surviving issue who are in the generation closest to you as well as any issue in that generation who predeceased you but who also were survived by their own issue.)

Example: If you are survived by two children but also gave birth to a third child who predeceased you and who left his or her own issue, your estate would be divided into three shares. Two-thirds would be distributed to your two living children and the other one-third would be distributed to the issue of your predeceased child.

✪ If you are survived by your spouse and no issue, your spouse will take your entire estate.

✪ If you are survived by issue and no spouse, your estate will go to your issue by representation.

✪ If you are not survived by a spouse or any issue but are survived by one or both of your parents, your estate will go to your surviving parent or parents.

✪ If you are not survived by a spouse, any issue, or by any of your parents, your estate will go to the issue of your deceased parents by representation.

✪ If you are not survived by any of the above people, there are additional rules for the distribution of your estate to your grandparents or to the issue of your grandparents if you are not survived by grandparents. (Consult the Estates, Powers and Trusts Law Section 4-1.1 for the specific rules.)

Example: Ebenezer dies without a will. Ebenezer was survived by two children, Tom and Joe. His wife and other two children, Anne and Rachelle had predeceased Ebenezer. However, Anne's two children and Rachelle's one child were living at the time of Ebenezer's death. Under New York law, Tom and Joe would inherit one-fourth each of Ebenezer's estate. The other one-half of his estate would be distributed evenly (one-sixth each) among Anne's two children and Rachelle's one child.

Probate Costs One more thing to note about dying without a will is that the probate of your estate can become more costly since there will be a need for court proceedings to determine who will be the *administrator* of your estate. An administrator has the same job as an executor if you leave a will appointing an executor. (see Chapter 3.) There will also be a need for court proceeding to determine the guardian of any of your minor children.

Out-of-State Wills

With respect to all of your personal property wherever it may be located, and with respect to all your real property located in New York, your out-of-state will is valid in New York. This is true even if it does not meet all the necessary procedures of New York for the valid signing of a will so long as the following is true. Your will must be *in writing*, *signed* by you, and *satisfy the laws* of the state in which you signed your will, or else satisfy the laws of the state in which you were domiciled either at the time you signed your will or at the time of your death.

Example: Jerry executed his will in State X which did not require that a testator publish the will (make it known to the witnesses that the document that the testator was signing was a will). With the laws of State X in mind, Jerry did not publish his will and later died in New York, leaving real property in New York and personal property in several states. Even though the will would not be valid under the procedures that New York requires for a validly executed will since it was not published, a New York court would accept the will for probate in New York because it was still validly executed in State X where it was signed. Thus, Jerry's out-of-state will is valid in New York.

What a Will Cannot Do

A will cannot direct that anything illegal be done and it cannot put unreasonable conditions on a gift. A provision that your daughter gets all of your property if she divorces her husband would be ignored by the court. She would get the property with no conditions attached. You can put some conditions in your will, to be sure they are enforceable, you should consult with an attorney.

Pets A will cannot leave money or property to an animal because animals cannot legally own property. If you wish to care for an animal after your death you should leave it in trust or to a friend whom you know will care for the animal.

Simple Wills

Any person who is eighteen or more years of age and of sound mind can make a will.

The wills in this book will pass your property whether your estate is $1,000 or $100,000,000. However, if your estate is over $1,500,00 (this amount will rise over the coming years as provided in the table on p.9), then you might be able to avoid *estate taxes* by using a trust or other tax-saving device. The larger your estate, the more you can save on estate taxes by doing more complicated planning. If you have a large estate and are concerned about estate taxes you should consult an estate planning attorney or a book on estate planning. There are also other times when a simple will may not meet your needs.

Will Contest If you expect that there may be a fight over your estate or that someone might contest your will's validity, you should consult a lawyer. If you leave less than the statutory share of your estate to your spouse or if you leave one or more of your children out of your will, it is likely that someone will contest your will.

Complicated Estates If you are the beneficiary of a trust or have any complications in your legal relationships, you may need special provisions in your will.

Blind or Unable to Write A person who is blind or who can sign only with an "X" should also consult a lawyer about the proper way to make and execute a will.

Large Estates If you expect to have over $1,500,000 (this amount is scheduled to rise, see table on p.9) at the time of your death, you may want to consult with a CPA or tax attorney regarding tax consequences.

Conditions If you wish to put some sort of conditions or restrictions on the property you leave you should consult a lawyer. For example, if you want to leave money to your brother only if he quits smoking or to a hospital only if they name a wing in your honor, you should consult an attorney to be sure that your conditions are valid in your state.

Using a Trust

Many people today elect to create trusts, particularly a type of trust called the *revocable living trust*. In a revocable living trust, the creator of the trust has control over the trust during his or her lifetime and can always revoke it if he or she chooses to do so. There are many reasons for using such trusts. One big reason is that any of your assets that are placed into the trust will pass by operation of the terms of the trust upon your death and thereby avoid probate altogether. This may save you money in terms of the fees that your estate must pay to probate property passing under your will.

Even if you choose to create a living trust, you still need a will. The reason you still need a will is that you want to make sure that you have a mechanism in place that will pass any property that you forget to include in your trust. A will does this. Without a will, any property that you mistakenly leave out of your trust will pass according to the laws of intestacy rather than according to your wishes.

3 MAKING A SIMPLE WILL

This chapter will teach you about various provisions that are typically included in a simple will. Most of the provisions discussed in this chapter are so standard and so important that they are included in every single form found in Appendix B. For example, you will see that no matter which form you choose to use in Appendix B, there is a clause naming an executor/executrix and a residuary clause. These two important clauses, along with other standard clauses included in every will, are explained in this chapter.

A few of the clauses covered in this chapter are *optional clauses* depending upon your own unique situation. For example, you do not need to include a clause about guardianship of your minor children if your children are all adults. If you turn to the outline on how to pick the right will for you on page 62, you will see that the form you choose for your own will depends on such optional clauses like a guardianship clause.

Even most attorneys use forms or templates when drafting a will. There is no reason why you can not do the same and choose one of the forms at the back of this book for your own will. But attorneys understand the significance of will provisions and so must you to properly make a will.

Remember that a will is a document that should reflect how you want your property divided up after you are deceased. To accurately dispose of your property as planned, you need to spend a little time now learning about the law with respect to will provisions. Once you have this knowledge, you can then choose and properly complete one of the forms contained in Appendix B or you can draft your own will if you so choose.

Identifying Parties in Your Will

When making your will, it is important to correctly identify the persons you name in your will. In some families, names differ only by middle initial or by Jr. or Sr. Be sure to check the names before you make your will. You can also add your relationship to the party, and their location such as "my cousin, Richard Harris of Albany, New York." The same applies to organizations and charities. For example, there are more than one group using the words "cancer society" or "heart association" in their names. Be sure to get the correct name of the group you intend to leave your gift.

Personal and Real Property

When the law speaks about *real property* it is talking about land and any structures (like your house) that you own on that land. The term personal property is really everything else. Because people acquire and dispose of *personal property* so often, it is not advisable to list a lot of small items in your will. Otherwise, when you sell or replace one of them you may have to rewrite your will.

One solution is to describe the *type* of item you wish to give. For example, instead of saying, "I leave my 2004 Ford to my sister," you should say, "I leave any automobile I own at the time of my death to my sister."

Of course, if you do mean to give a specific item you should describe it. For example instead of "I leave my diamond ring to Joan," you should say, "I leave to Joan the one-half carat diamond ring that I inherited from my grandmother," because you might own more than one diamond ring at the time of your death.

Personal property can include a wide variety of things like cash that you may own in various bank accounts, stocks or bonds (sometimes called securities), annuities, pensions, IRAs, and even insurance proceeds that may be payable to you upon your death. You want to make sure that every single thing you own is disposed according to your wishes under your will. One way to do this is to spell out in your will the name of the person(s) who are to inherit property under your will and exactly what it is that you want them to inherit. You will learn how to make such *testamentary gifts* in the following section.

Another way to dispose of your assets is to have a general blanket provision called a *residuary clause* where you simply state that *all the rest of my property that I have not specifically given away be given to so and so.* You will learn about residuary clause following the section on testamentary gifts. Both types of provisions (testamentary provisions and residuary clauses) are usually included in wills together. As you will learn, residuary clauses are always included in a will.

Making Testamentary Gifts

When you make gifts under your will (testamentary gifts), you are said to *bequeath* personal property and to *devise* real property. For example, if you wanted to give your house to your daughter, you could state in your will "I devise my dwelling house and premises described as 201 Washington Avenue, Albany, New York to my daughter, Anne Huges, together with all policies of fire, burglary, property damage, and other insurance thereon."

Bequests of personal property can be made in three ways. The first way is through a *specific* bequest in which you employ language that distinguishes the personal property that you are giving from all other property in your estate. To make a specific bequest, you should employ the word "my" before the property that you are giving away under your will. For example, if you state in your will "I give and bequeath to Anne Murray my 100 shares of IBM stock," you have made a specific bequest.

On the other hand, if you were to state "I give and bequeath to Anne Murray 100 shares of IBM stock" without employing the word "my," you will have made a *general* instead of *specific* bequest.

A third way to give away personal property is called a *demonstrative* bequest. A demonstrative gift is a mix between a specific and general bequest. When you make a demonstrative gift, you are making a general gift out of a specific part of your estate. The statement, "I give and bequeath the sum of $1,000 to be paid out of the proceeds of the sale of a sufficient number of my IBM stock," would be a demonstrative gift.

Order of Distribution

While the differences between specific, general, and demonstrative gifts of your personal property may seem minute, these different types of bequests have significance in the law. You should first note that when you make a specific bequest of property, that property will only go to your designated beneficiary under the terms of your will if such property exists in your estate at the time of your death. Thus if you make a specific bequest of "100 shares of my IBM stock," there must be IBM shares of stock for your beneficiary to be able to take any such shares. If you have sold this particular stock prior to your death, the gift is said to *adeem* and your beneficiary would not inherit anything under your will. By making your gift specific, the law says that those specific shares of IBM stock must exist on the date of your death.

On the other hand, if you make a general or demonstrative bequest of the same 100 shares, your beneficiary would still be able to inherit the value of 100 shares of IBM stock even if these specific shares had previously been sold prior to your death. This is true because general and demonstrative bequests are paid out of the general assets of your estate.

Gifts with Debt

With respect to the consequence of specific, general, and demonstrative bequests, there is a second point that you should note. If the assets in your estate are not large enough to satisfy all of the administrative expenses and gifts under your will, general bequests will be used to meet these liabilities before demonstrative and specific gifts unless you provide otherwise in your will. Thus, if you are concerned that your estate will not be large enough to meet all of your bequests in your will, and you desire, for example, that your daughter take her bequest at the expense of your bequest to your personal friend, Tom, you would need to add a provision in your will like "in the event that my estate shall prove insufficient to pay my bequests provided herein in full, I direct my executor to apply my estate first to the payment in full of the bequest to my daughter and second to the payment of my bequest to my friend, Tom."

One last point: your beneficiary will take not only any property that you devise or bequeath, but also any liens to which the property is subject, unless you provide otherwise in your will. For example, if you devise your residence to your spouse, that residence will be subject to any mortgages that still exist on the property. A way to provide otherwise in your will would be to state "if at the time of my death, the devise of my residence to my spouse shall be subject to any lien, security interest, or other charge, the same shall be paid out of my residuary estate and the said devisee shall receive the same free and clear of any such lien." Of course by making such a statement, you must realize that other beneficiaries under your residuary estate would have to give up their inheritance to pay off any such mortgage.

Residuary Clause

A *residuary clause* is the clause in your will by which you name one or more persons to take all "the rest and residue" of your estate. Any time that you make testamentary gifts in your will to specific persons, you should also include a residuary clause to dispose of any other property that you may own at the time of your death. If you do not include a residuary clause, any property that you have not specifically given away under the terms of your will falls into *intestacy*.

Example: Bob created a will leaving all of his "earthly belongings" to his wife with no provision covering the situation where his wife predeceased him. Bob died after the death of his wife and he had not changed his will. All of Bob's property passed outside his will according to the laws of intestacy. Bob could have avoided this problem by providing for a substituted beneficiary and by using a residuary clause.

Wills often make specific gifts of a testator's property and then include a residuary clause in which the bulk of the testator's estate goes to close relatives. One important thing to keep in mind when creating such a will is the possibility that your estate may decline in value. This may result in your specific testamentary gifts taking up a large proportion of your estate and leaving little or no property to your close relatives under the residuary clause. To counteract this problem, it is advisable to use percentages or fractions when making bequests of your property to ensure that the persons named in your residuary clause inherit the largest portion of your estate.

Example: At the time Anne made her will, her estate was worth $300,000. Anne wanted very much to give each of her three nieces $15,000 and to give the rest of her estate to her two children. Anne created a will specifically giving her three nieces $15,000 each and gave the "rest, residue and remainder" of her estate to her children. At the time of Anne's death, her estate was worth only $45,000 due to unexpected health care costs. Under the terms of her will, each of the three nieces would inherit $15,000 leaving no property to pass to her children. Anne could have avoided this problem by giving each of her three nieces five percent or one-twentieth of her estate in which case her three nieces would have taken only $2,250 of her estate with the remaining $38,250 to be divided among her children.

If you feel compelled to make specific testamentary gifts of a certain dollar value rather than by using fractions or percentages, you should remember to make changes to your will if your assets change.

Living Trusts If you are using your will in conjunction with a living trust that you have created, you may want to provide that your residuary estate pass to the trustee of your living trust. This way any property that you have forgotten to place in your trust during your lifetime will end up in your trust after your death. To be extra cautious, you should include alternative provisions for how you want your property to pass just in case your living trust is deemed ineffective for some reason at the time of your death. For example, you could add to your will the provision "if for any reasons my trust is not effective at the time of my death, my residuary estate should pass to _____."

The _____ would be the place to put the mirror terms of your trust of how you intended your property to pass. This way you absolutely ensure that the same people you intended to pass your property under trust will be the same people who inherit under your will if for some reason your trust is not effective at the time of your death.

Alternate Beneficiaries

You should always provide for an *alternate beneficiary* in case the person you name dies before you and you do not have a chance to make out a new will. If you do not the gift is said to *lapse*. In such a case, New York's *anti-lapse statute* kicks in and determines who gets the property.

Survivor or Descendants

Suppose your will leaves your property to your sister and brother; however, your brother predeceases you. Should his share go to your sister or to your brother's children or grandchildren?

If you are giving property to two or more persons and you want it all to go to the other if one of them dies, you would specify "or the survivor of them."

If, on the other hand, you want the property to go to the children of the deceased person, you should state in your will "or their lineal descendants." This would include his or her children and grandchildren.

Family or Person

If you decide you want it to go to your brother's children and grandchildren, you must next decide if an equal share should go to each family or to each person. For example: your brother leaves three grandchildren; one is an only child of his daughter and the others are the children of his son. Should all grandchildren get equal shares or should they take their parent's share?

When you want each family to get an equal share it is called *per stirpes*. When you want each person to get an equal share it is called *per capita*. Most of the wills in this book use per stirpes because that is the most common way property is left. If you wish to leave your property per capita then you can rewrite the will with this change.

Example: Alice leaves her property to her two daughters, Mary and Pat in equal shares, or to their lineal descendants per stirpes. Her daughter, Pat, predeceases Alice, leaving two children. Mary would receive one half of the estate and Pat's two children will receive the other half of the estate. In this case, if Alice had chosen per capita, Mary and the grandchildren would have each received one third of the estate.

Per Stirpes Distribution

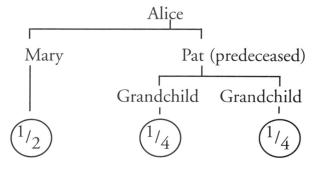

Per Capita Distribution

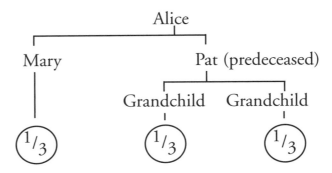

There are fourteen different will forms in this book, but you may want to divide your property slightly differently from what these forms state. If so, you can retype the forms according to these rules, specifying whether the property should go to the *survivor* or the *lineal descendants*. If this is confusing to you, consider seeking the advice of an attorney.

Survivorship

Many people put a clause in their will stating that anyone receiving property under the will must survive for thirty days (or forty-five or sixty) after the death of the deceased. This is so that if the two people die in the same accident there will not be two probates and the property will not go to the other party's heirs.

Example: Fred and Wilma were married and each had children by previous marriages. They did not have survivorship clauses in their wills and they were in an airplane crash. Fred's children hired several expert witnesses and a large law firm to prove that at the time of the crash Fred lived for a few minutes longer than Wilma. That way when Wilma died first, all of her property went to Fred. When he died a few minutes later, all of Fred and Wilma's property went to his children. Wilma's children received nothing.

Guardians

If you have minor children you should name a guardian for them. There are two types of guardians, a guardian over the *person* and a guardian over the *property*. The first is the person who decides where the children will live and makes the other parental decisions for them. A guardian of the property is in charge of the minor's property and inheritance. In most cases, one person is appointed guardian of both the person and property. But some people prefer the children to live with one person, but to have the money held by another person.

Example: Sandra was a widow with a young daughter. She knew that if anything happened to her, her sister would be the best person to raise her daughter. But her sister was never good with money. So when Sandra made out her will, she named her sister as guardian over the person of her daughter and she named her father as guardian over the estate of her daughter.

When naming a guardian, it is always advisable to name an alternate guardian in case your first choice is unable to serve for any reason.

Children's Trust

When a parent dies leaving a minor child and the child's property is held by a guardian, the guardianship ends when the child reaches the age of 18 and all of the property is turned over to the child. Most parents do not feel their children are competent at the age of 18 to handle large sums of money and prefer that it be held until the child is 21, 25, 30 or even older.

If you wish to set up a complicated system of deciding when your children should receive various amounts of your estate, you should consult a lawyer to draft a trust. However, if you want a simple provision that you want the funds held to a higher age than 18 and you have someone you trust to make decisions about paying for education or other expenses for your child or children, you can put that provision in your will as a children's trust.

The children's trust trustee can be the same person as the guardian or a different person. It is advisable to name an alternate trustee if your first choice is unable to handle it.

Your Executor or Executrix

An *executor* is the person who will be in charge of your probate. When your designated executor is a female, she is called your *executrix*. You may appoint more than one executor or executrix of your will. Your choice of an executor/executrix is perhaps the most significant decision you will make in your will. He or she will gather your assets, handle the sale of them if necessary, prepare an inventory, hire an attorney, and distribute the property. Any person who is not under eighteen, incompetent, or a felon is eligible to be your executor. Some possible choices include a beneficiary under your will, your attorney, or a close friend. In any case, you should choose a person you trust. You should also be aware that whoever you choose as an executor is entitled to payment (called a *commission*) for their services which is paid directly out of your estate.

Some people like to name two persons as executors to avoid jealously or because they may want one of their executors who is skilled in business matters to serve along with another who lacks such skills. However, you should be aware that this can be time-consuming when it comes time to probate your estate since both executors must sign all necessary papers and there can be problems if your executors do not agree on something.

This being said, you may want to consider naming more than one executor if you have a large estate which runs the possibility of incurring estate taxes (i.e., one which exceeds the amounts listed in the table on p.9). This is because every executor you name is entitled to a *commission* for his or her services, which is paid from your estate. Such commissions are deductible when it comes to figuring out estate taxes. Thus for people with large estates, naming two or more beneficiaries (like their children) as joint executors could be a way to reduce any estate taxes.

It is recommended to provide that your executor does not have to post any bond in any jurisdiction for the faithful performance of his or her duties. Otherwise, a bond may be required to be posted. You should also give your executor the power to borrow. If you have any business that you are going to pass under your will, you should also give your executor power to continue the business. Otherwise, your executor will have to go to court to get permission to run the business. This will simply increase the expense your estate will incur in obtaining this court permission.

If you neglect to appoint an executor in your will or your appointed executor/executrix fails to qualify for some reason, then the court must appoint someone to perform the duties of an executor. This person is referred to as an *administrator with the will annexed* or *administrator c.t.a.* for short. Only certain persons are eligible to apply for the position.

If you are interested in learning about who can qualify, you should consult the *Surrogate's Court Procedure Act*, Section 1418. The Surrogate's Court Procedure Act, usually abbreviated SCPA, can be found in the law library at any law school or court library in New York state. You will probably also be able to find it in the law section of a public library. It deals mainly with how your estate is handled after you die (i.e., presentation of your will to the court for probate, payment of taxes, etc.) and is a subject beyond the scope of this book.

Witnesses

A will must be witnessed by *two* persons to be valid in New York. In Vermont, three witnesses are required, so if you own real property in Vermont you should have three witnesses to your will.

It is a good idea to place before the signatures of your witnesses a clause that sets forth the performance of all the requirements to a validly executed will. This clause is called an *attestation clause* and is included in all the forms in this book.

The witnesses you choose to witness your will should *not* be any persons who are beneficiaries under your will. In other words, if you have given a person any property under your will, you should make sure that such a person does not serve as a witness to your will. While the witnessing by a person who is a beneficiary under your will does not invalidate your will, such a witness will not be able to take your property given to him under your will as you have intended.

Handwritten Wills   In some states, a will that is entirely handwritten (called a *holographic will*) is valid if there are no witnesses. However, in New York, even a handwritten will needs a witness.

Self-Proving Clause

Even if no person objects to the probate of your will after your death, a court will require that the two witnesses to your will come to court in order to be examined about the genuineness of your will and its proper execution. This procedure is called *proving the will*. It can be a time-consuming and costly procedure since your witnesses must be located and various procedures must be followed if such witnesses can no longer be located or do not exist. However, if you have each of your two witnesses sign a clause, called a *self-proving clause*, before a notary public that your will was executed with all the required formalities, this sworn statement may be accepted by the court in place of the production of each of your attesting witnesses at the time of your death. The net result is to save your estate a lot of hassle and money. (see form 17, p.97.)

Disinheriting Someone

As discussed in Chapter 2, certain people, like your spouse and children, will inherit under your will according to various percentages by operation of law if you have no will. The whole point of having a will is so that you can alter such provisions and pass the property according to your own wishes. For example, you may want to give your son Jon some more money than your sister Annette or vice versa. However there may be a time when you want to disinherit one of these natural beneficiaries completely and leave him or her nothing.

When it comes to disinheriting a natural beneficiary like a child completely you need to be a little careful. As covered in Chapter 1, it may be impossible to eliminate a spouse from inheriting a percentage of your estate due to a spouse's *elective share* right. Additionally, in the case of a child, you need to be careful if your true intention is to eliminate that child from inheriting any property under your estate. The reason for this is that such a child is likely to *contest* your will at the time of your death and argue that you some how mistakenly forgot to include him or her in your will.

Perhaps the best way to leave a child out of your will if this is your true intention is to leave a *token bequest* to that child in your will (say $500). This way such a child will have a harder time arguing that you mistakenly left him or her out of your will since you really did include that person in your will. To go a step further, you can include in your will a provision that if any person challenges your will that person will loose the specific bequest under your will.

Funeral Arrangements

You have the right to determine the *manner of burial* of your body after your death. This right includes the right to be cremated. However, since your will may not be read until after your body has been buried, it is advisable to let your family know about your wishes. You should express your wishes clearly in the manner that you desire and insert this clause directly into your will. Here are two examples of possible clauses that could be inserted into your will.

(1) *I direct my funeral be conducted by* _____ (name of funeral agency) *according to the rites of the* _____ (name of church)*, and that my remains be interred in the plot owned by me* _____ (name of cemetery) *in the county of* _____ *of New York.*

(2) *I direct that my body shall be cremated and that my ashes be disposed of as my wife shall deem fitting.*

Forms

There are fourteen different **WILL** forms included in this book for easy use. You can cut them out, photocopy them, or retype them on plain paper.

The forms in this book are printed on both sides of the page. If you photocopy them on separate pages or type your will on more than one piece of paper you should staple the pages together, initial each page and have both witnesses initial each page. Each page should state at the bottom, "page 1 of 3," "page 2 of 3," etc.

Corrections

Your will should have no white-outs or erasures. If for some reason it is impossible to make a will without corrections, they should be initialed by you and both witnesses.

4 | EXECUTING A WILL

The signing of a will is a serious legal event and must be done properly or the will may be declared invalid. Preferably, it should be done in a private room without distraction. All parties must watch each other sign and no one should leave the scene until all have signed.

Example: Phil brought over a folded document and told his good friends that it was his will and that he needed his friends to be witnesses. The friends agreed and signed in the appropriate blank spaces but never saw Phil sign his will. After Phil's death, the surrogate court refused to probate Phil's will because the witnesses testified that they had never actually seen Phil sign his will. Phil's property passed to persons not named in his will through the *law of intestacy*.

Procedure

After reading the will, you (the testator) should assemble at least two witnesses who will not be beneficiaries under your will. You should state, "This is my will. I have read it and I understand it and this is how I want it to read. I want you two people to be my witnesses." You should next read the *attestation clause* (the clause just above the blanks where the witnesses sign) out loud. You must next date and sign your name at the end of the will in full view of the witnesses. You must next request that the witnesses sign their respective names and addresses below your signature.

After your witnesses have signed as attesting witnesses under your name, it is highly recommended that you have the witnesses sign an affidavit with a *self-proving clause*. (see Chapter 3.) This will enable the will to be probated at the time of your death without having to bring your witnesses to court. In order to properly complete the affidavit, you will need each of your attesting witnesses to sign the affidavit before a notary public. The notary public should not be one of your two witnesses. Never have any *interested people* (persons who will inherit any property under your will) in the room.

Copies   It is a good idea to make at least one copy of your will, but you should not personally sign or notarize the copies. The execution of copies of your will can create problems for your estate. For example, the loss of one of the executed copies of a will creates a presumption that possibly you destroyed your will. This possibility prevents the probate of the will because of the lack of proof that you did not intend to destroy your will.

Example: Ed typed up his will in triplicate consisting of a ribbon copy and two carbon copies. Ed executed all three copies of the will, keeping the two carbon copies at his home and the one ribbon copy at his attorney's office. Upon Ed's death, no one could locate the carbon copies at Ed's home. A large court battle subsequently ensued over whether Ed's ribbon copy could be probated. Since the carbon copies were in Ed's exclusive control and could not be located, there was a presumption that Ed destroyed these copies and since all the executed copies constituted Ed's will, the court held that the revocation of any one of them revoked the other.

Ed could have avoided the subsequent battle over his will if he had executed only one copy of his will. If Ed had executed only one copy instead of the two others, the destruction of this one copy would have clearly shown his intention to revoke his will and there may not have been subsequent litigation over whether he intended to probate the executed copy held by his attorney. The lesson is the following—unexecuted copies of your will are fine, but you should only store one copy of your will with your signature on it.

5   After You Sign Your Will

The chapter discusses a few important things to do or to remember after you have signed your will. The chapter starts off on how to properly store your will and then discusses what to do if you want to make changes to your will or revoke it altogether. Lastly, the chapter discusses events that may occur in your life that affect the provisions of your will such as a divorce.

Storing Your Will

You should keep your will in a place safe from fire and easily accessible to your heirs. Your executor should know of its whereabouts or you may risk that no one will discover your will after you die. You should note that if you decide to keep your will in a safe-deposit box that a court order will be required to obtain that will after your death.

Another possible place to keep your will is with the surrogate court (the court that will be used to probate your will) in your county of residence. By statute, the surrogate court must accept your will for safekeeping and the court will give you a receipt acknowledging that you have deposited your will with the court. However, before the court will accept your will, you must seal your will in an envelope and write the day, month, and year that you have deposited your will on the sealed envelope. Although certain surrogate courts such as the one in Albany county do not charge a fee for storing your will, you need to check with the court of your county since a fee may be charged. After your death, the surrogate court will open your will and file it in the court.

Revoking Your Will

Once you have made a will you may *revoke* it or may direct someone else to revoke it in your presence. This may be done by burning, tearing, cutting, cancellation, obliteration, or by other mutilation or destruction of your will.

Example: Ralph tells his son Clyde to go to the basement safe and tear up his (Ralph's) will. If Clyde does not tear it up in Ralph's presence it is probably not effectively revoked.

You may also revoke your will by properly executing a will or codicil at a later time stating that you expressly revoke your earlier will. You should note that if you make a later will and do not include a clause expressly revoking your earlier will, your earlier will is not revoked. The first will's provisions will be effective to the extent that they are consistent with your new will.

If you need to revoke your will that is filed with the surrogate court, you need to physically go to the court and sign a log book. Make sure you bring identification and a sealed envelope with the name of the will, the date of the will, and the names of the witnesses. If you cannot go to surrogate court (for example, if you are in the hospital), then you can revoke your will by executing a new will that revokes it.

Revival If you change your will by drafting a new one and later decide you do not like the changes and want to go back to your old will, you cannot simply destroy the new one and revive the old one. Once you execute a new will revoking an old one, you cannot revive the old one unless you execute a new document stating that you intend to revive the old will. In other words, you might as well execute a new will.

Changing Your Will

You should not make any changes on your will after it has been signed. If you wish to change some provision of your will, you can do it by executing a document called a *codicil*. A person may make an unlimited number of codicils to a will, but each one must be executed with the same formality of a will and should be self-proved. Therefore, it is usually better to just prepare a new will than to prepare codicils. If you wish to prepare a **CODICIL** to your will, then you can use the form included in this book. (see form 18, p.99.)

Effect of Divorce on Your Will

You should note that a divorce, annulment, declaration of nullity, or dissolution of your marriage revokes any appointment of property made in your will to your former spouse as well as any provision naming your former spouse as an executor or trustee unless your will contains a provision stating that this result should not be the case. However, events like divorce do not invalidate your will. Your will is simply probated as though your former spouse predeceased you.

6 MAKING A LIVING WILL, HEALTH CARE PROXY, AND POWER OF ATTORNEY

After your will has been executed is a good time to execute a *living will, health care proxy,* and *durable power of attorney.* How to prepare these three documents is the subject of this chapter.

Living Will

A *living will* is a document in which one states, while in good health, what measures he or she does not want used to extend one's life when one is dying. Although the New York Legislature has not yet adopted a statute recognizing the validity of a living will, New York courts have upheld your right to make such a document and to thereby decline certain medical treatment by artificial means and devices while in a terminally ill state or condition. A living will may also be a good backup if your *health care proxy* is unavailable for some reason.

A form that you can use as a **LIVING WILL** is included in Appendix B. (see form 20, p.103.) The execution of such a form by you is a personal decision. You can use this form or create your own form. In either case, you should be specific about what type of treatments you do not want should you reach a terminal state. The document will speak for you should you later be incompetent and in a terminally ill condition.

In order to properly execute a living will, you should sign the document in the presence of at least two witnesses eighteen years of age or older, who must also sign the document.

Health Care Proxy

Related to the living will (but which is statutorily recognized) is a *health care proxy*. This document gives someone you designate the power to make medical or other health care decisions for you. Any competent adult can create a health care proxy by signing and dating the proxy in the presence of the two adult witnesses who must make these decisions either in accordance with your wishes or if such wishes are not reasonably known, then in accordance with your best interests. However, if your views regarding artificial nutrition and hydration are not reasonably known, then the agent will not have the authority to make those types of decisions. So you should expressly state your desires with respect to artificial nutrition and hydration in the proxy in order for your agent to act according to your wishes. Further information on health care proxies can also be found in the *Power of Attorney Handbook*, by Edward A. Haman, published by Sourcebooks, Inc. A form that you can use as a **HEALTH CARE PROXY** is included in Appendix B. (see form 21, p.105.)

Examples of medical treatments about which you may wish to give your agent special instructions include:

- ✪ artificial respiration;

- ✪ artificial nutrition and hydration (nourishment and water provided by feeding tube);

- ✪ cardiopulmonary resuscitation (CPR); and,

- ✪ dialysis.

As stated, unless your agent knows your wishes about artificial nutrition and hydration (nourishment and water provided by a feeding tube), he or she will

7 | MAKING ANATOMICAL GIFTS

Any person of sound mind who is eighteen years old or older can donate all or any part of his or her body for scientific research or transplantation. Unless you indicate otherwise, consent to make *anatomical gifts* may also be given by a relative of a deceased person. However, because relatives are often in shock or too upset to make such a decision, it is better to have one's intent made clear before death.

Procedure

The easiest way for a person to express his or her consent to make anatomical gifts is by signing the back side of his or her New York state license stating that you are willing to be considered as an organ donor. Your signature must be made in the presence of two witnesses who must also sign their names.

Consent to make anatomical gifts can also be made in the will. New York law provides that such gifts become effective immediately on death without the necessity of probating the will and even despite the invalidity of a will.

Revoking   If you change your mind and later do not wish to make any anatomical gift, you can amend or revoke your decision. If a document or will has been delivered to a specified donee, it may be amended or revoked in the following ways:

- ✪ by executing and delivering a signed statement to the donee;

- ✪ by an oral statement of revocation made in the presence of two persons, communicated to the donee;

- ✪ by a statement made during a terminal illness to an attending physician and communicated to the donee; or,

- ✪ by a signed card or document found on the person of the donor or in his or her effects. A **UNIFORM DONOR CARD** is included in this book. (see form 23, p.111.)

If any document of gift has not been delivered to a donee, it may be revoked by any of the above methods or by destruction, cancellation, or mutilation of the document and all executed copies of the document.

GLOSSARY

A

administrator (**administratrix** if female). A person appointed by the court to oversee distribution of the property of someone who died (either without a will or if the person designated in the will is unable to serve).

attested will. A will that includes an attestation clause and has been signed in front of witnesses.

B

beneficiary. A person who is entitled to receive property from a person who died (regardless of whether there is a will).

bequest. Personal property left to someone in a will.

C

children's trust. A trust set up to hold property given to children. Usually it provides that the children will not receive their property until they reach a higher age than the age of majority.

codicil. An amendment to a will.

community property. Property acquired by a husband and wife by their labors during their marriage.

D

decedent. A person who has died.

descendent. A child, grandchild, great-grandchild, etc.

devise. Real property left to someone in a will. A person who is entitled to a devise is called a *devisee*.

E

elective share. In noncommunity property states, the portion of the estate that may be taken by a surviving spouse, regardless of what the will says.

executor (**executrix** if female). A person appointed in a will to oversee distribution of the property of someone who died with a will.

exempt property. Property that is exempt from distribution as a normal part of the estate.

F

family allowance. An amount of money set aside from the estate to support the family of the decedent for a period of time.

forced share. *See elective share.*

H

heir. A person who will inherit from a decedent who died without a will.

holographic will. A will in which all of the material provisions are entirely in the handwriting on the maker. Holographic wills are not legal if not witnessed.

I

intestate. Without making a will. One who dies without a will is said to have *died intestate.*

intestate share. In noncommunity property states, the portion of the estate a spouse is entitled to receive if there is no will.

J

joint tenancy. A type of property ownership by two or more persons, in which if one owner dies, that owner's interest goes to the other joint tenants (not to the deceased owner's heirs as in tenancy in common).

L

legacy. Real property left to someone in a will. A person who is entitled to a legacy is called a *legatee.*

living will. A document expressing the writer's desires regarding how medical care is to be handled in the event the writer is not able to express his or her wishes concerning the use of life-prolonging medical procedures.

P

per capita. Distribution of property with equal shares going to each person.

per stirpes. Distribution of property with equal shares going to each family line.

personal representative. A person appointed by the court, or will, to oversee distribution of the property of the person who died. This is a more modern term than "administrator," "executor," etc., and applies regardless of whether there is a will.

probate. The process of settling a decedent's estate through the probate court.

R

residue. The property that is left over in an estate after all specific bequests and devises.

S

self-proving affidavit. A form added to a will in which the will maker and witnesses state under oath that they have signed and witnessed the will.

specific bequest *or* **specific devise.** A gift in a will of a specific item of property or a specific amount of cash.

statutory will. A will that has been prepared according to the requirements of a statute.

T

tenancy by the entirety. A type of property ownership by a married couple, in which the property automatically passes to one spouse upon the death of the other. This is basically the same as joint tenancy, except that it is only between a husband and wife.

tenancy in common. Ownership of property by two or more people, in which each owner's share would descend to that owner's heirs (not to the other owners as in joint tenancy).

testate. With a will. One who dies with a will is said to have *died testate*.

testator (**testatrix** if female). A person who makes his or her will.

testamentary substitute. The giving away of property during a person's life in the form of joint tenancies, revocable trusts, or gifts, in order to avoid his/her spouse receiving an elective share.

APPENDIX A
SAMPLE WILLS AND FORMS

The following pages include sample filled-in forms for some of the wills in this book. They are filled out in different ways for different situations. You should look at all of them to see how the different sections can be filled in. Only one example of a self-proved will affidavit is shown, but you should use it with every will.

Last Will and Testament

I, _____John Smith_____ a resident of _____Tioga_____ County, New York do hereby make, publish, and declare this to be my Last Will and Testament, hereby revoking any and all Wills and Codicils heretofore made by me.

FIRST: I direct that all my just debts and funeral expenses be paid out of my estate as soon after my death as is practicable.

SECOND: I give, devise, and bequeath the following specific gifts: the gold watch which I got from my grandfather to my brother Ned Smith.

THIRD: I give, devise, and bequeath the rest, residue and remainder of my estate, real, personal, and mixed, of whatever kind and wherever situated, of which I may die seized or possessed, or in which I may have any interest or over which I may have any power of appointment or testamentary disposition, to my spouse, _____Barbara Smith_____. If my said spouse does not survive me, I give, devise and bequeath the said property to my sisters, Jan Smith, Joan Smith, and Jennifer Smith in equal shares _____, or the survivor of them.

FOURTH: In the event that any beneficiary fails to survive me by thirty days, then this will shall take effect as if that person had predeceased me.

FIFTH: I hereby nominate, constitute, and appoint _____Barbara Smith_____ as Executor/Executrix of this, my Last Will and Testament. In the event that such named person is unable or unwilling to serve at any time or for any reason, then I nominate, constitute, and appoint _____Reginald Smith_____ as Executor/Executrix in the place and stead of the person first named herein. It is my will and I direct that my Executor/Executrix shall not be required to furnish a bond for the faithful performance of his or her duties in any jurisdiction, any provision of law to the contrary notwithstanding, and I give my Executor/Executrix full power to administer my estate, including the power to settle claims, to borrow, pay debts, and sell, lease or exchange real and personal property without court order.

IN WITNESS WHEREOF, I declare this to be my Last Will and Testament and execute it willingly as my free and voluntary act for the purposes expressed herein and I am of legal age and sound mind and make this under no constraint or undue influence, this _29th_ day of January, 2004 at _____Oswego_____ State of _____New York_____.

_____*John Smith*_____ L.S.

The foregoing instrument was on said date subscribed at the end thereof by
_____John Smith_____, the above named Testator who signed, published, and declared this instrument to be his/her Last Will and Testament in the presence of us and each of us, who thereupon at his/her request, in his/her presence, and in the presence of each other, have hereunto subscribed our names as witnesses thereto. We are of sound mind and proper age to witness a will and understand this to be his/her will, and to the best of our knowledge testator is of legal age to make a will, of sound mind, and under no constraint or undue influence.

_____*Brenda Jones*_____residing at_____Oswego, New York_____

_____*John Doe*_____residing at_____Ithaca, New York_____

Last Will and Testament

I, _____ John Smith _____ a resident of _____ Tioga _____
County, New York do hereby make, publish, and declare this to be my Last Will and Testament, hereby revoking any and all Wills and Codicils heretofore made by me.

FIRST: I direct that all my just debts and funeral expenses be paid out of my estate as soon after my death as is practicable.

SECOND: I give, devise, and bequeath the following specific gifts:
10 shares of Applebee's stock to my aunt, Martha Brown --------------------
----

THIRD: I give, devise, and bequeath the rest, residue and remainder of my estate, real, personal, and mixed, of whatever kind and wherever situated, of which I may die seized or possessed, or in which I may have any interest or over which I may have any power of appointment or testamentary disposition, to my spouse, _ Barbara Smith --------------------. If my said spouse does not survive me, I give, devise and bequeath the said property to my children _ Amy Smith, _____
Beamy Smith, and Seamy Smith--
-- ,
in equal shares or to their lineal descendants, per stirpes.

FOURTH: In the event that any beneficiary fails to survive me by thirty days, then this will shall take effect as if that person had predeceased me.

FIFTH: I hereby nominate, constitute, and appoint _____ Barbara Smith _____ as Executor/Executrix of this, my Last Will and Testament. In the event that such named person is unable or unwilling to serve at any time or for any reason, then I nominate, constitute, and appoint _____ Reginald Smith _____ as Executor/Executrix in the place and stead of the person first named herein. It is my will and I direct that my Executor/Executrix shall not be required to furnish a bond for the faithful performance of his or her duties in any jurisdiction, any provision of law to the contrary notwithstanding, and I give my Executor/Executrix full power to administer my estate, including the power to settle claims, to borrow, pay debts, and sell, lease or exchange real and personal property without court order.

IN WITNESS WHEREOF, I declare this to be my Last Will and Testament and execute it willingly as my free and voluntary act for the purposes expressed herein and I am of legal age and sound mind and make this under no constraint or undue influence, this _5th_ day of _January_, 2004 at _____ Oswego _____ State of _____ New York _____.

John Smith
_____ L.S.

The foregoing instrument was on said date subscribed at the end thereof by

_____ John Smith _____, the above named Testator who signed, published, and declared this instrument to be his/her Last Will and Testament in the presence of us and each of us, who thereupon at his/her request, in his/her presence, and in the presence of each other, have hereunto subscribed our names as witnesses thereto. We are of sound mind and proper age to witness a will and understand this to be his/her will, and to the best of our knowledge testator is of legal age to make a will, of sound mind, and under no constraint or undue influence.

_____*Brenda Jones*_____residing at____Oswego, New York_____

_____*John Doe*_____residing at____Ithaca, New York_____

Last Will and Testament

I, _____Lester Doe_____ a resident of _____Westchester_____ County, New York do hereby make, publish, and declare this to be my Last Will and Testament, hereby revoking any and all Wills and Codicils heretofore made by me.

FIRST: I direct that all my just debts and funeral expenses be paid out of my estate as soon after my death as is practicable.

SECOND: I give, devise, and bequeath the following specific gifts:

None ---

THIRD: I give, devise, and bequeath the rest, residue and remainder of my estate, real, personal, and mixed, of whatever kind and wherever situated, of which I may die seized or possessed, or in which I may have any interest or over which I may have any power of appointment or testamentary disposition, to my children _____ James Doe, Mary Doe, Larry Doe, Barry Doe, Carrie Doe, and Moe Doe--------- --- _____, plus any afterborn or adopted children in equal shares or to their lineal descendants per stirpes.

FOURTH: In the event that any beneficiary fails to survive me by thirty days, then this will shall take effect as if that person had predeceased me.

FIFTH: In the event any of my children have not attained the age of 18 years at the time of my death, I hereby nominate, constitute, and appoint _____Herbert Doe_____ ------------------ as guardian over the person of any of my children who have not reached the age of majority at the time of my death. In the event that said guardian is unable or unwilling to serve, then I nominate, constitute, and appoint _____Tom Doe -------------------- as guardian. Said guardian shall serve without bond or surety.

SIXTH: In the event any of my children have not attained the age of 18 years at the time of my death, I hereby nominate, constitute, and appoint _____Missy Doe_____ ------------------ as guardian over the estate of any of my children who have not reached the age of majority at the time of my death. In the event that said guardian is unable or unwilling to serve, then I nominate, constitute, and appoint _____Joanna Doe ------------------_____ as guardian. Said guardian shall serve without bond or surety.

SEVENTH: I hereby nominate, constitute, and appoint _____Clarence Doe_____ as Executor/Executrix of this, my Last Will and Testament. In the event that such named person is unable or unwilling to serve at any time or for any reason, then I nominate, constitute, and appoint _____Englebert Doe_____ as Executor/Executrix in the place and stead of the person first named herein. It is my will and I direct that my Executor/Executrix shall not be required to furnish a bond for the faithful performance of his or her duties in any jurisdiction, any provision of law to the contrary notwithstanding, and I give my Executor/Executrix full power to administer my estate, including the power to settle claims, to borrow, pay debts, and sell, lease or exchange real and personal property without court order.

IN WITNESS WHEREOF, I declare this to be my Last Will and Testament and execute it willingly as my free and voluntary act for the purposes expressed herein and I am of legal age and sound mind and make this under no constraint or undue influence, this __2nd__ day of __July__, 2004 at __White Plains__ State of _____New York_____.

_____*John Doe*_____L.S.

The foregoing instrument was on said date subscribed at the end thereof by _____John Doe_____, the above named Testator who signed, published, and declared this instrument to be his/her Last Will and Testament in the presence of us and each of us, who thereupon at his/her request, in his/her presence, and in the presence of each other, have hereunto subscribed our names as witnesses thereto. We are of sound mind and proper age to witness a will and understand this to be his/her will, and to the best of our knowledge testator is of legal age to make a will, of sound mind, and under no constraint or undue influence.

____*Jane Roe*____residing at___White Plains, New York___

____*Melvin Coe*____residing at___Yonkers, New York___

Last Will and Testament

I, _____ Mary Smith _____ a resident of _____ Westchester _____

County, New York do hereby make, publish, and declare this to be my Last Will and Testament,
hereby revoking any and all Wills and Codicils heretofore made by me.

FIRST: I direct that all my just debts and funeral expenses be paid out of my estate as soon
after my death as is practicable.

SECOND: I give, devise, and bequeath the following specific gifts:
my various kitchen utensils, including but not limited to, my 12-piece
Baker's Secret pan set to my daughter, Janey Walters.---------------------
----

THIRD: I give, devise, and bequeath the rest, residue and remainder of my estate, real, personal,
and mixed, of whatever kind and wherever situated, of which I may die seized or possessed, or in
which I may have any interest or over which I may have any power of appointment or testamentary
disposition, to the following: _____ House in Vermont to grandson, Ralph Walters.------
----

--,

or to the survivor of them.

FOURTH: In the event that any beneficiary fails to survive me by thirty days, then this will
shall take effect as if that person had predeceased me.

FIFTH: I hereby nominate, constitute, and appoint _____ Regina Walters _____ as
Executor/Executrix of this, my Last Will and Testament. In the event that such named person is
unable or unwilling to serve at any time or for any reason, then I nominate, constitute, and appoint
_____ Tom Doe _____ as Executor/Executrix in the place and stead of the person
first named herein. It is my will and I direct that my Executor/Executrix shall not be required to furnish a bond for the faithful performance of his or her duties in any jurisdiction, any provision of law
to the contrary notwithstanding, and I give my Executor/Executrix full power to administer my
estate, including the power to settle claims, to borrow, pay debts, and sell, lease or exchange real and
personal property without court order.

IN WITNESS WHEREOF, I declare this to be my Last Will and Testament and execute it
willingly as my free and voluntary act for the purposes expressed herein and I am of legal age and
sound mind and make this under no constraint or undue influence, this __6th__ day of
__May__, __2004__ at _____ White Plains _____ State of _____ New York _____.

_____ *Mary Smith* _____ L.S.

The foregoing instrument was on said date subscribed at the end thereof by
_____Mary Smith_____, the above named Testator who signed, published, and declared this instrument to be his/her Last Will and Testament in the presence of us and each of us, who thereupon at his/her request, in his/her presence, and in the presence of each other, have hereunto subscribed our names as witnesses thereto. We are of sound mind and proper age to witness a will and understand this to be his/her will, and to the best of our knowledge testator is of legal age to make a will, of sound mind, and under no constraint or undue influence.

_____*Leon Brown*_____residing at____New York City, New York_____

_____*Mildred Brown*_____residing at____Huntington Station, New York___

_____*Manuela Jacobs*_____residing at___New York City, New York_____

(**NOTE:** *Because the testator owns property in Vermont and that state requires three witnesses, an additional witness line has been added.*)

Self-Proved Will Affidavit
(attach to Will)

STATE OF NEW YORK

COUNTY OF ___Westchester___

    Each of the undersigned, individually and severally being duly sworn deposes and says:

    The within will was subscribed in our presence and sight at the end thereof by _____John Doe_____, the within named testat__or___, on the __5th_____ day of ___July,_____, __2004__, at _____three_____ o'clock.

    Said testat__or__ at the time of making such subscription declared the instrument so subscribed to be h_is_ last will.

    Each of the undersigned thereupon signed h_er/his_name as a witness at the end of said will at the request of said testat_or_____ and in h_is_ presence and sight and in the presence and sight of each other.

    Said testat_or____ was, at the time of so executing said will, over the age of 18 years and, in the respective opinions of the undersigned, of sound mind, memory and understanding and not under any restraint or in any respect incompetent to make a will.

    The testat_or____, in the respective opinions of the undersigned, could read, write and converse in the English language and was suffering from no defect of sight, hearing or speech, or from any other physical or mental impairment which would affect h_is_ capacity to make a valid will. The will was executed as a single, original instrument and was not executed in counterparts.

    Each of the undersigned was acquainted with said testat_or_____ at such time and makes this affidavit at h_is_ request.

    The within will was shown to the undersigned at the time this affidavit was made, and was examined by each of them as to the signature of said testat_____ and of the undersigned.

                               ___*Jane Roe*_____(Witness)

                                 ___*Melvin Coe*_____(Witness)

Subscribed, sworn and acknowledged before me by _____John Doe_____, the testator, and by _____Melvin Coe_____ and ___Jane Roe_____ _____, witnesses, this _5th__ day of __July, 2004_____.

_____*C.U. Sine*_____

Notary or other officer

Codicil to the Will of

_____ Larry Lowe _____

I, _____ Larry Lowe _____, a resident of _____ Leon _____ County, New York declare this to be the first codicil to my Last Will and Testament dated _____ July 5 _____, __2001__.

FIRST: I hereby revoke the clause of my Will which reads as follows:
FOURTH: I hereby leave $5000.00 to my daughter Mildred --------------------
----

---.

SECOND: I hereby add the following clause to my Will: _____
FOURTH: I hereby leave $1000.00 to my daughter Mildred --------------------
----

---.

THIRD: In all other respects I hereby confirm and republish my Last Will and Testament dated _____ July 5 _____, __2001__.

IN WITNESS WHEREOF, I have signed, published, and declared the foregoing instrument as and for a codicil to my Last Will and Testament, this __5th__ day of _____ January _____, __2004__.

_____ *Larry Lowe*

The foregoing instrument was on the __5th__ day of _____ January _____, __2004__, signed at the end thereof, and at the same time published and declared by _____ Larry Lowe _____, as and for a codicil to his/her Last Will and Testament, dated _____ July 5 _____, __2001__, in the presence of each of us, who, this attestation clause having been read to us, did at the request of the said testator/testatrix, in his/her presence and in the presence of each other signed our names as witnesses thereto.

James Smith _____ residing at __ Binghamton, New York _____

Mary Smith _____ residing at __ Elmira, New York _____

Living Will

Declaration made this ___29___ day of ___January___, ___2004___. I, ___Norman Milquetoast___, willfully and voluntarily make known my desire that my dying not be artificially prolonged under the circumstances set forth below, and I do hereby declare:

If at any time I have a terminal condition and if my attending or treating physician and another consulting physician have determined that there can be no medical probability of my recovery from such condition, I direct that life-prolonging procedures be withheld or withdrawn when the application of such procedures would serve only to prolong artificially the process of dying, and that I be permitted to die naturally with only the administration of medication or the performance of any medical procedure deemed necessary to provide me with comfort, care or alleviate pain.

It is my intention that this declaration be honored by my family and physician as the final expression of my legal right to refuse medical or surgical treatment and to accept the consequences for such refusal.

This authorization includes (X) does not include ( ) the withholding or withdrawal of artificial feeding and hydration (check only one box above).

Special Instructions (if any) _____ None. ------------------------------------
----

Signed this ___29th___ day of ___January___, ___2004___.

Norman Milquetoast
Signature
Address: ___1234 New York Avenue___
___South Nyack, NY 10961___

I understand the full import of this declaration, and am emotionally and mentally competent to make this declaration.

Additional instructions (optional):
None --

Norman Milquetoast
(Signed)

Harvey Nabor
Witness
___1236 New York Avenue___
___South Nyack, NY 10961___
Address
___914-555-2121___
Phone

June Nabor
Witness
___1236 New York Avenue___
___South Nyack, NY 10961___
Address
___914-555-2121___
Phone

APPENDIX B
FORMS

The following pages contain forms that can be used to prepare a will, codicil, living will, health care proxy, durable power of attorney, and Uniform Donor Card. They should only be used by persons who have read this book, who do not have any complications in their legal affairs, and who understand the forms they are using. The forms may be used right out of the book or they may be photocopied or retyped.

How to Pick the Right Will

Follow the chart and use the form number in the black circle,
then use Form 17, the self-proving affidavit.

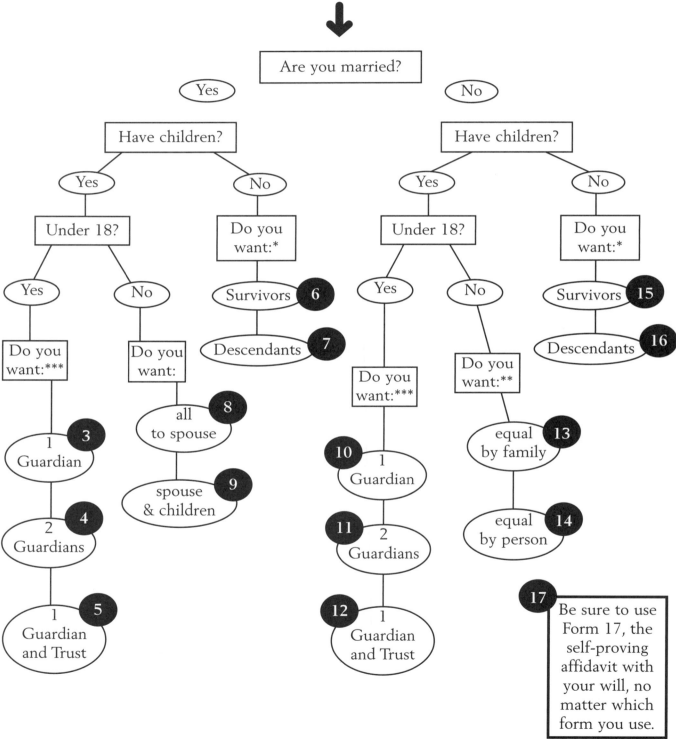

*For an explanation of survivors/descendants, see page 23.

**For an explanation of families/persons, see page 23.

*** For an explanation of children's guardians and trust, see page 25.

_____
_____
_____
_____
_____
_____

Other Property (trusts, partnerships, businesses, profit sharing, copyrights, etc.)

_____
_____
_____
_____
_____
_____
_____
_____

Liabilities

Real Estate Loans

_____
_____
_____
_____
_____
_____
_____

Vehicle Loans

_____
_____
_____
_____
_____
_____
_____

Other Secured Loans

_____
_____
_____
_____
_____

_____
_____

Unsecured Loans and Debts (taxes, child support, judgments, etc.)

_____
_____
_____
_____
_____
_____
_____
_____

Beneficiary List

Name_____ Address_____ Phone_____

_____
_____
_____
_____
_____
_____
_____
_____

Last Will and Testament

I, _____ a resident of _____ County, New York do hereby make, publish, and declare this to be my Last Will and Testament, hereby revoking any and all Wills and Codicils heretofore made by me.

FIRST: I direct that all my just debts and funeral expenses be paid out of my estate as soon after my death as is practicable.

SECOND: I give, devise, and bequeath the following specific gifts:

_____

_____

_____

THIRD: I give, devise, and bequeath the rest, residue and remainder of my estate, real, personal, and mixed, of whatever kind and wherever situated, of which I may die seized or possessed, or in which I may have any interest or over which I may have any power of appointment or testamentary disposition, to my spouse, _____. If my said spouse does not survive me, I give, devise and bequeath the said property to my children

_____

_____

_____, plus any afterborn or adopted children in equal shares or their lineal descendants, per stirpes.

FOURTH: In the event that any beneficiary fails to survive me by thirty days, then this will shall take effect as if that person had predeceased me.

FIFTH: Should my spouse not survive me, I hereby nominate, constitute, and appoint _____ as guardian over the person and estate of any of my children who have not reached the age of majority at the time of my death. In the event that said guardian is unable or unwilling to serve, then I nominate, constitute, and appoint _____ as guardian. Said guardian shall serve without bond or surety.

SIXTH: I hereby nominate, constitute, and appoint _____ _____ as Executor/Executrix of this, my Last Will and Testament. In the event that such named person is unable or unwilling to serve at any time or for any reason, then I nominate, constitute, and appoint _____ as Executor/Executrix in the place and stead of the person first named herein. It is my will and I direct that my Executor/Executrix shall not be required to furnish a bond for the faithful performance of his or her duties in any jurisdiction, any provision of law to the contrary notwithstanding, and I give my Executor/Executrix full power to administer my estate, including the power to settle claims, to borrow, pay debts, and sell, lease or exchange real and personal property without court order.

IN WITNESS WHEREOF, I declare this to be my Last Will and Testament and execute it willingly as my free and voluntary act for the purposes expressed herein and I am of legal age and sound mind and make this under no constraint or undue influence, this _____ day of _____, _____ at _____ State of _____.

_____L.S.

The foregoing instrument was on said date subscribed at the end thereof by _____, the above named Testator who signed, published, and declared this instrument to be his/her Last Will and Testament in the presence of us and each of us, who thereupon at his/her request, in his/her presence, and in the presence of each other, have hereunto subscribed our names as witnesses thereto. We are of sound mind and proper age to witness a will and understand this to be his/her will, and to the best of our knowledge testator is of legal age to make a will, of sound mind, and under no constraint or undue influence.

_____ residing at _____

_____ residing at _____

Last Will and Testament

I, _____ a resident of _____
County, New York do hereby make, publish, and declare this to be my Last Will and Testament, hereby revoking any and all Wills and Codicils heretofore made by me.

FIRST: I direct that all my just debts and funeral expenses be paid out of my estate as soon after my death as is practicable.

SECOND: I give, devise, and bequeath the following specific gifts:
_____
_____
_____
_____

THIRD: I give, devise, and bequeath the rest, residue and remainder of my estate, real, personal, and mixed, of whatever kind and wherever situated, of which I may die seized or possessed, or in which I may have any interest or over which I may have any power of appointment or testamentary disposition, to my spouse, _____.
If my said spouse does not survive me, I give, devise and bequeath the said property to my children
_____
_____
_____, plus any afterborn or adopted children in equal shares or their lineal descendants, per stirpes.

FOURTH: In the event that any beneficiary fails to survive me by thirty days, then this will shall take effect as if that person had predeceased me.

FIFTH: Should my spouse not survive me, I hereby nominate, constitute, and appoint _____, as guardian over the person of any of my children who have not reached the age of majority at the time of my death. In the event that said guardian is unable or unwilling to serve, then I nominate, constitute, and appoint _____ _____ as guardian. Said guardian shall serve without bond or surety.

SIXTH: Should my spouse not survive me, I hereby nominate, constitute, and appoint _____ as guardian over the estate of any of my children who have not reached the age of majority at the time of my death. In the event that said guardian is unable or unwilling to serve, then I nominate, constitute, and appoint _____ _____ as guardian. Said guardian shall serve without bond or surety.

SEVENTH: I hereby nominate, constitute, and appoint _____ _____ as Executor/Executrix of this, my Last Will and Testament. In the event that such named person is unable or unwilling to serve at any time or for any reason, then I nominate, constitute, and appoint _____ as Executor/Executrix in the place and stead of the person first named herein. It is my will and I direct that my Executor/Executrix shall not be required to furnish a bond for the faithful performance of his or her duties in any jurisdiction, any provision of law to the contrary notwithstanding, and I give my Executor/Executrix full power to administer my estate, including the power to settle claims, to borrow, pay debts, and sell, lease or exchange real and personal property without court order.

IN WITNESS WHEREOF, I declare this to be my Last Will and Testament and execute it willingly as my free and voluntary act for the purposes expressed herein and I am of legal age and sound mind and make this under no constraint or undue influence, this _____ day of _____, _____ at _____ State of _____.

_____L.S.

The foregoing instrument was on said date subscribed at the end thereof by _____, the above named Testator who signed, published, and declared this instrument to be his/her Last Will and Testament in the presence of us and each of us, who thereupon at his/her request, in his/her presence, and in the presence of each other, have hereunto subscribed our names as witnesses thereto. We are of sound mind and proper age to witness a will and understand this to be his/her will, and to the best of our knowledge testator is of legal age to make a will, of sound mind, and under no constraint or undue influence.

_____ residing at _____

_____ residing at _____

Last Will and Testament

I, _____ a resident of _____ County, New York do hereby make, publish, and declare this to be my Last Will and Testament, hereby revoking any and all Wills and Codicils heretofore made by me.

FIRST: I direct that all my just debts and funeral expenses be paid out of my estate as soon after my death as is practicable.

SECOND: I give, devise, and bequeath the following specific gifts:

_____

_____

_____

THIRD: I give, devise, and bequeath the rest, residue and remainder of my estate, real, personal, and mixed, of whatever kind and wherever situated, of which I may die seized or possessed, or in which I may have any interest or over which I may have any power of appointment or testamentary disposition, to my spouse, _____. If my said spouse does not survive me, I give, devise and bequeath the said property to my children

_____

_____

_____, plus any afterborn or adopted children in equal shares or their lineal descendants, per stirpes.

FOURTH: In the event that any beneficiary fails to survive me by thirty days, then this will shall take effect as if that person had predeceased me.

FIFTH: In the event that any of my children have not reached the age of _____ years at the time of my death, then the share of any such child shall be held in a separate trust by _____ for such child.

The trustee shall use the income and that part of the principal of the trust as is, in the trustee's sole discretion, necessary or desirable to provide proper housing, medical care, food, clothing, entertainment and education for the trust beneficiary, considering the beneficiary's other resources. Any income that is not distributed shall be added to the principal. Additionally, the trustee shall have all powers conferred by the law of the state having jurisdiction over this trust, as well as the power to pay from the assets of the trust reasonable fees necessary to administer the trust.

The trust shall terminate when the child reaches the age specified above and the remaining assets distributed to the child, unless they have been exhausted sooner. In the event the child dies prior to the termination of the trust, then the assets shall pass to the estate of the child. The interests of the beneficiary under this trust shall not be assignable and shall be free from the claims of creditors to the full extent allowed by law.

In the event the said trustee is unable or unwilling to serve for any reason, then I nominate, constitute, and appoint _____as alternate trustee. No bond shall be required of either trustee in any jurisdiction and this trust shall be administered without court supervision as allowed by law.

SIXTH: Should my spouse not survive me, I hereby nominate, constitute, and appoint _____as guardian over the person and estate of any of my children who have not reached the age of majority at the time of my death. In the event that said guardian is unable or unwilling to serve, then I nominate, constitute, and appoint _____ as guardian.

SEVENTH: I hereby nominate, constitute, and appoint _____ _____ as Executor/Executrix of this, my Last Will and Testament. In the event that such named person is unable or unwilling to serve at any time or for any reason, then I nominate, constitute, and appoint _____ as Executor/Executrix in the place and stead of the person first named herein. It is my will and I direct that my Executor/Executrix shall not be required to furnish a bond for the faithful performance of his or her duties in any jurisdiction, any provision of law to the contrary notwithstanding, and I give my Executor/Executrix full power to administer my estate, including the power to settle claims, to borrow, pay debts, and sell, lease or exchange real and personal property without court order.

IN WITNESS WHEREOF, I declare this to be my Last Will and Testament and execute it willingly as my free and voluntary act for the purposes expressed herein and I am of legal age and sound mind and make this under no constraint or undue influence, this _____ day of _____, _____ at _____ State of _____.

_____L.S.

The foregoing instrument was on said date subscribed at the end thereof by _____, the above named Testator who signed, published, and declared this instrument to be his/her Last Will and Testament in the presence of us and each of us, who thereupon at his/her request, in his/her presence, and in the presence of each other, have hereunto subscribed our names as witnesses thereto. We are of sound mind and proper age to witness a will and understand this to be his/her will, and to the best of our knowledge testator is of legal age to make a will, of sound mind, and under no constraint or undue influence.

_____ residing at _____

_____ residing at _____

Last Will and Testament

I, _____ a resident of _____
County, New York do hereby make, publish, and declare this to be my Last Will and Testament, hereby revoking any and all Wills and Codicils heretofore made by me.

FIRST: I direct that all my just debts and funeral expenses be paid out of my estate as soon after my death as is practicable.

SECOND: I give, devise, and bequeath the following specific gifts:
_____
_____
_____

THIRD: I give, devise, and bequeath the rest, residue and remainder of my estate, real, personal, and mixed, of whatever kind and wherever situated, of which I may die seized or possessed, or in which I may have any interest or over which I may have any power of appointment or testamentary disposition, to my spouse, _____. If my said spouse does not survive me, I give, devise and bequeath the said property to
_____
_____
_____, or the survivor of them.

FOURTH: In the event that any beneficiary fails to survive me by thirty days, then this will shall take effect as if that person had predeceased me.

FIFTH: I hereby nominate, constitute, and appoint _____ as Executor/Executrix of this, my Last Will and Testament. In the event that such named person is unable or unwilling to serve at any time or for any reason, then I nominate, constitute, and appoint _____ as Executor/Executrix in the place and stead of the person first named herein. It is my will and I direct that my Executor/Executrix shall not be required to furnish a bond for the faithful performance of his or her duties in any jurisdiction, any provision of law to the contrary notwithstanding, and I give my Executor/Executrix full power to administer my estate, including the power to settle claims, to borrow, pay debts, and sell, lease or exchange real and personal property without court order.

IN WITNESS WHEREOF, I declare this to be my Last Will and Testament and execute it willingly as my free and voluntary act for the purposes expressed herein and I am of legal age and sound mind and make this under no constraint or undue influence, this _____ day of _____, _____ at _____ State of _____.

_____L.S.

The foregoing instrument was on said date subscribed at the end thereof by _____ , the above named Testator who signed, published, and declared this instrument to be his/her Last Will and Testament in the presence of us and each of us, who thereupon at his/her request, in his/her presence, and in the presence of each other, have hereunto subscribed our names as witnesses thereto. We are of sound mind and proper age to witness a will and understand this to be his/her will, and to the best of our knowledge testator is of legal age to make a will, of sound mind, and under no constraint or undue influence.

_____ residing at _____

_____ residing at _____

Last Will and Testament

I, _____ a resident of _____

County, New York do hereby make, publish, and declare this to be my Last Will and Testament, hereby revoking any and all Wills and Codicils heretofore made by me.

FIRST: I direct that all my just debts and funeral expenses be paid out of my estate as soon after my death as is practicable.

SECOND: I give, devise, and bequeath the following specific gifts:

_____

_____

_____

THIRD: I give, devise, and bequeath the rest, residue and remainder of my estate, real, personal, and mixed, of whatever kind and wherever situated, of which I may die seized or possessed, or in which I may have any interest or over which I may have any power of appointment or testamentary disposition, to my spouse, _____. If my said spouse does not survive me, I give, devise and bequeath the said property to_____

_____ , _____

_____ , or to their lineal descendants, per stirpes.

FOURTH: In the event that any beneficiary fails to survive me by thirty days, then this will shall take effect as if that person had predeceased me.

FIFTH: I hereby nominate, constitute, and appoint _____ as Executor/Executrix of this, my Last Will and Testament. In the event that such named person is unable or unwilling to serve at any time or for any reason, then I nominate, constitute, and appoint _____ as Executor/Executrix in the place and stead of the person first named herein. It is my will and I direct that my Executor/Executrix shall not be required to furnish a bond for the faithful performance of his or her duties in any jurisdiction, any provision of law to the contrary notwithstanding, and I give my Executor/Executrix full power to administer my estate, including the power to settle claims, to borrow, pay debts, and sell, lease or exchange real and personal property without court order.

IN WITNESS WHEREOF, I declare this to be my Last Will and Testament and execute it willingly as my free and voluntary act for the purposes expressed herein and I am of legal age and sound mind and make this under no constraint or undue influence, this _____ day of _____ , _____ at _____ State of _____ .

_____ L.S.

The foregoing instrument was on said date subscribed at the end thereof by _____, the above named Testator who signed, published, and declared this instrument to be his/her Last Will and Testament in the presence of us and each of us, who thereupon at his/her request, in his/her presence, and in the presence of each other, have hereunto subscribed our names as witnesses thereto. We are of sound mind and proper age to witness a will and understand this to be his/her will, and to the best of our knowledge testator is of legal age to make a will, of sound mind, and under no constraint or undue influence.

_____ residing at _____

_____ residing at _____

Last Will and Testament

I, _____ a resident of _____ County, New York do hereby make, publish, and declare this to be my Last Will and Testament, hereby revoking any and all Wills and Codicils heretofore made by me.

FIRST: I direct that all my just debts and funeral expenses be paid out of my estate as soon after my death as is practicable.

SECOND: I give, devise, and bequeath the following specific gifts:

_____

_____

_____

THIRD: I give, devise, and bequeath the rest, residue and remainder of my estate, real, personal, and mixed, of whatever kind and wherever situated, of which I may die seized or possessed, or in which I may have any interest or over which I may have any power of appointment or testamentary disposition, as follows:

_____% to my spouse, _____ and

_____% to my children, _____

_____

_____,

in equal shares or to their lineal descendants per stirpes.

FOURTH: In the event that any beneficiary fails to survive me by thirty days, then this will shall take effect as if that person had predeceased me.

FIFTH: I hereby nominate, constitute, and appoint _____ as Executor/Executrix of this, my Last Will and Testament. In the event that such named person is unable or unwilling to serve at any time or for any reason, then I nominate, constitute, and appoint _____ as Executor/Executrix in the place and stead of the person first named herein. It is my will and I direct that my Executor/Executrix shall not be required to furnish a bond for the faithful performance of his or her duties in any jurisdiction, any provision of law to the contrary notwithstanding, and I give my Executor/Executrix full power to administer my estate, including the power to settle claims, to borrow, pay debts, and sell, lease or exchange real and personal property without court order.

IN WITNESS WHEREOF, I declare this to be my Last Will and Testament and execute it willingly as my free and voluntary act for the purposes expressed herein and I am of legal age and sound mind and make this under no constraint or undue influence, this _____ day of _____, _____ at _____ State of _____.

_____ L.S.

The foregoing instrument was on said date subscribed at the end thereof by _____ , the above named Testator who signed, published, and declared this instrument to be his/her Last Will and Testament in the presence of us and each of us, who thereupon at his/her request, in his/her presence, and in the presence of each other, have hereunto subscribed our names as witnesses thereto. We are of sound mind and proper age to witness a will and understand this to be his/her will, and to the best of our knowledge testator is of legal age to make a will, of sound mind, and under no constraint or undue influence.

_____ residing at _____

_____ residing at _____

Last Will and Testament

I, _____ a resident of _____

County, New York do hereby make, publish, and declare this to be my Last Will and Testament, hereby revoking any and all Wills and Codicils heretofore made by me.

FIRST: I direct that all my just debts and funeral expenses be paid out of my estate as soon after my death as is practicable.

SECOND: I give, devise, and bequeath the following specific gifts:

_____

_____

_____

THIRD: I give, devise, and bequeath the rest, residue and remainder of my estate, real, personal, and mixed, of whatever kind and wherever situated, of which I may die seized or possessed, or in which I may have any interest or over which I may have any power of appointment or testamentary disposition, to my children _____

_____

_____

_____, plus any afterborn or adopted children in equal shares or to their lineal descendants per stirpes.

FOURTH: In the event that any beneficiary fails to survive me by thirty days, then this will shall take effect as if that person had predeceased me.

FIFTH: In the event any of my children have not attained the age of 18 years at the time of my death, I hereby nominate, constitute, and appoint _____ _____ as guardian over the person and estate of any of my children who have not reached the age of majority at the time of my death. In the event that said guardian is unable or unwilling to serve, then I nominate, constitute, and appoint _____ _____ as guardian. Said guardian shall serve without bond or surety.

SIXTH: I hereby nominate, constitute, and appoint _____ _____ as Executor/Executrix of this, my Last Will and Testament. In the event that such named person is unable or unwilling to serve at any time or for any reason, then I nominate, constitute, and appoint _____ as Executor/Executrix in the place and stead of the person first named herein. It is my will and I direct that my Executor/Executrix shall not be required to furnish a bond for the faithful performance of his or her duties in any jurisdiction, any provision of law to the contrary notwithstanding, and I give my Executor/Executrix full power to administer my estate, including the power to settle claims, to borrow, pay debts, and sell, lease or exchange real and personal property without court order.

IN WITNESS WHEREOF, I declare this to be my Last Will and Testament and execute it willingly as my free and voluntary act for the purposes expressed herein and I am of legal age and sound mind and make this under no constraint or undue influence, this _____ day of _____, _____ at _____ State of _____.

_____L.S.

The foregoing instrument was on said date subscribed at the end thereof by _____, the above named Testator who signed, published, and declared this instrument to be his/her Last Will and Testament in the presence of us and each of us, who thereupon at his/her request, in his/her presence, and in the presence of each other, have hereunto subscribed our names as witnesses thereto. We are of sound mind and proper age to witness a will and understand this to be his/her will, and to the best of our knowledge testator is of legal age to make a will, of sound mind, and under no constraint or undue influence.

_____ residing at _____

_____ residing at _____

Last Will and Testament

I, _____ a resident of _____ County, New York do hereby make, publish, and declare this to be my Last Will and Testament, hereby revoking any and all Wills and Codicils heretofore made by me.

FIRST: I direct that all my just debts and funeral expenses be paid out of my estate as soon after my death as is practicable.

SECOND: I give, devise, and bequeath the following specific gifts:

_____

_____

_____

THIRD: I give, devise, and bequeath the rest, residue and remainder my estate, real, personal, and mixed, of whatever kind and wherever situated, of which I may die seized or possessed, or in which I may have any interest or over which I may have any power of appointment or testamentary disposition, to my children _____

_____

_____

_____, plus any afterborn or adopted children in equal shares or to their lineal descendants per stirpes.

FOURTH: In the event that any beneficiary fails to survive me by thirty days, then this will shall take effect as if that person had predeceased me.

FIFTH: In the event any of my children have not attained the age of 18 years at the time of my death, I hereby nominate, constitute, and appoint _____ _____ as guardian over the person of any of my children who have not reached the age of majority at the time of my death. In the event that said guardian is unable or unwilling to serve, then I nominate, constitute, and appoint _____ as guardian. Said guardian shall serve without bond or surety.

SIXTH: In the event any of my children have not attained the age of 18 years at the time of my death, I hereby nominate, constitute, and appoint _____ _____ as guardian over the estate of any of my children who have not reached the age of majority at the time of my death. In the event that said guardian is unable or unwilling to serve, then I nominate, constitute, and appoint _____ as guardian. Said guardian shall serve without bond or surety.

SEVENTH: I hereby nominate, constitute, and appoint _____ as Executor/Executrix of this, my Last Will and Testament. In the event that such named person is unable or unwilling to serve at any time or for any reason, then I nominate, constitute, and appoint _____ as Executor/Executrix in the place and stead of the person first named herein. It is my will and I direct that my Executor/Executrix shall not be required to furnish a bond for the faithful performance of his or her duties in any jurisdiction, any provision of law to the contrary notwithstanding, and I give my Executor/Executrix full power to administer my estate, including the power to settle claims, to borrow, pay debts, and sell, lease or exchange real and personal property without court order.

IN WITNESS WHEREOF, I declare this to be my Last Will and Testament and execute it willingly as my free and voluntary act for the purposes expressed herein and I am of legal age and sound mind and make this under no constraint or undue influence, this _____ day of _____, _____ at _____ State of _____.

_____L.S.

The foregoing instrument was on said date subscribed at the end thereof by _____, the above named Testator who signed, published, and declared this instrument to be his/her Last Will and Testament in the presence of us and each of us, who thereupon at his/her request, in his/her presence, and in the presence of each other, have hereunto subscribed our names as witnesses thereto. We are of sound mind and proper age to witness a will and understand this to be his/her will, and to the best of our knowledge testator is of legal age to make a will, of sound mind, and under no constraint or undue influence.

_____ residing at _____

_____ residing at _____

Last Will and Testament

I, _____ a resident of _____ County, New York do hereby make, publish, and declare this to be my Last Will and Testament, hereby revoking any and all Wills and Codicils heretofore made by me.

FIRST: I direct that all my just debts and funeral expenses be paid out of my estate as soon after my death as is practicable.

SECOND: I give, devise, and bequeath the following specific gifts:

_____

_____

_____

THIRD: I give, devise, and bequeath the rest, residue and remainder of my estate, real, personal, and mixed, of whatever kind and wherever situated, of which I may die seized or possessed, or in which I may have any interest or over which I may have any power of appointment or testamentary disposition, to my children _____

_____

_____

_____, plus any afterborn or adopted children in equal shares or to their lineal descendants per stirpes.

FOURTH: In the event that any beneficiary fails to survive me by thirty days, then this will shall take effect as if that person had predeceased me.

FIFTH: In the event that any of my children have not reached the age of _____ years at the time of my death, then the share of any such child shall be held in a separate trust by _____ for such child.

The trustee shall use the income and that part of the principal of the trust as is, in the trustee's sole discretion, necessary or desirable to provide proper housing, medical care, food, clothing, entertainment and education for the trust beneficiary, considering the beneficiary's other resources. Any income that is not distributed shall be added to the principal. Additionally, the trustee shall have all powers conferred by the law of the state having jurisdiction over this trust, as well as the power to pay from the assets of the trust reasonable fees necessary to administer the trust.

The trust shall terminate when the child reaches the age specified above and the remaining assets distributed to the child, unless they have been exhausted sooner. In the event the child dies prior to the termination of the trust, then the assets shall pass to the estate of the child. The interests of the beneficiary under this trust shall not be assignable and shall be free from the claims of creditors to the full extent allowed by law.

In the event the said trustee is unable or unwilling to serve for any reason, then I nominate, constitute, and appoint _____as alternate trustee. No bond shall be required of either trustee in any jurisdiction and this trust shall be administered without court supervision as allowed by law.

SIXTH: In the event any of my children have not attained the age of 18 years at the time of my death, I hereby nominate, constitute, and appoint _____ as guardian over the person and estate of any of my children who have not reached the age of majority at the time of my death. In the event that said guardian is unable or unwilling to serve, then I nominate, constitute, and appoint _____ as guardian. Said guardian shall serve without bond or surety.

SEVENTH: I hereby nominate, constitute, and appoint _____ as Executor/Executrix of this, my Last Will and Testament. In the event that such named person is unable or unwilling to serve at any time or for any reason, then I nominate, constitute, and appoint _____ as Executor/Executrix in the place and stead of the person first named herein. It is my will and I direct that my Executor/Executrix shall not be required to furnish a bond for the faithful performance of his or her duties in any jurisdiction, any provision of law to the contrary notwithstanding, and I give my Executor/Executrix full power to administer my estate, including the power to settle claims, to borrow, pay debts, and sell, lease or exchange real and personal property without court order.

IN WITNESS WHEREOF, I declare this to be my Last Will and Testament and execute it willingly as my free and voluntary act for the purposes expressed herein and I am of legal age and sound mind and make this under no constraint or undue influence, this _____ day of _____, _____ at _____ State of _____.

_____L.S.

The foregoing instrument was on said date subscribed at the end thereof by _____, the above named Testator who signed, published, and declared this instrument to be his/her Last Will and Testament in the presence of us and each of us, who thereupon at his/her request, in his/her presence, and in the presence of each other, have hereunto subscribed our names as witnesses thereto. We are of sound mind and proper age to witness a will and understand this to be his/her will, and to the best of our knowledge testator is of legal age to make a will, of sound mind, and under no constraint or undue influence.

_____ residing at _____

_____ residing at _____

Last Will and Testament

I, _____ a resident of _____ County, New York do hereby make, publish, and declare this to be my Last Will and Testament, hereby revoking any and all Wills and Codicils heretofore made by me.

FIRST: I direct that all my just debts and funeral expenses be paid out of my estate as soon after my death as is practicable.

SECOND: I give, devise, and bequeath the following specific gifts:

_____

_____

_____

THIRD: I give, devise, and bequeath the rest, residue and remainder of my estate, real, personal, and mixed, of whatever kind and wherever situated, of which I may die seized or possessed, or in which I may have any interest or over which I may have any power of appointment or testamentary disposition, to my children _____

_____

_____

_____, in equal shares, or their lineal descendants per stirpes.

FOURTH: In the event that any beneficiary fails to survive me by thirty days, then this will shall take effect as if that person had predeceased me.

FIFTH: I hereby nominate, constitute, and appoint _____ _____ as Executor/Executrix of this, my Last Will and Testament. In the event that such named person is unable or unwilling to serve at any time or for any reason, then I nominate, constitute, and appoint _____ as Executor/Executrix in the place and stead of the person first named herein. It is my will and I direct that my Executor/Executrix shall not be required to furnish a bond for the faithful performance of his or her duties in any jurisdiction, any provision of law to the contrary notwithstanding, and I give my Executor/Executrix full power to administer my estate, including the power to settle claims, to borrow, pay debts, and sell, lease or exchange real and personal property without court order.

IN WITNESS WHEREOF, I declare this to be my Last Will and Testament and execute it willingly as my free and voluntary act for the purposes expressed herein and I am of legal age and sound mind and make this under no constraint or undue influence, this _____ day of _____, _____ at _____ State of _____.

_____L.S.

The foregoing instrument was on said date subscribed at the end thereof by _____, the above named Testator who signed, published, and declared this instrument to be his/her Last Will and Testament in the presence of us and each of us, who thereupon at his/her request, in his/her presence, and in the presence of each other, have hereunto subscribed our names as witnesses thereto. We are of sound mind and proper age to witness a will and understand this to be his/her will, and to the best of our knowledge testator is of legal age to make a will, of sound mind, and under no constraint or undue influence.

_____ residing at _____

_____ residing at _____

Last Will and Testament

I, _____ a resident of _____ County, New York do hereby make, publish, and declare this to be my Last Will and Testament, hereby revoking any and all Wills and Codicils heretofore made by me.

FIRST: I direct that all my just debts and funeral expenses be paid out of my estate as soon after my death as is practicable.

SECOND: I give, devise, and bequeath the following specific gifts:
_____
_____
_____

THIRD: I give, devise, and bequeath the rest, residue and remainder of my estate, real, personal, and mixed, of whatever kind and wherever situated, of which I may die seized or possessed, or in which I may have any interest or over which I may have any power of appointment or testamentary disposition, to my children _____
_____
_____
_____, in equal shares, or their lineal descendants per capita.

FOURTH: In the event that any beneficiary fails to survive me by thirty days, then this will shall take effect as if that person had predeceased me.

FIFTH: I hereby nominate, constitute, and appoint _____ _____ as Executor/Executrix of this, my Last Will and Testament. In the event that such named person is unable or unwilling to serve at any time or for any reason, then I nominate, constitute, and appoint _____ as Executor/Executrix in the place and stead of the person first named herein. It is my will and I direct that my Executor/Executrix shall not be required to furnish a bond for the faithful performance of his or her duties in any jurisdiction, any provision of law to the contrary notwithstanding, and I give my Executor/Executrix full power to administer my estate, including the power to settle claims, to borrow, pay debts, and sell, lease or exchange real and personal property without court order.

IN WITNESS WHEREOF, I declare this to be my Last Will and Testament and execute it willingly as my free and voluntary act for the purposes expressed herein and I am of legal age and sound mind and make this under no constraint or undue influence, this _____ day of _____, _____ at _____ State of _____.

_____L.S.

The foregoing instrument was on said date subscribed at the end thereof by
_____, the above named Testator who signed, published,
and declared this instrument to be his/her Last Will and Testament in the presence of us and each of
us, who thereupon at his/her request, in his/her presence, and in the presence of each other, have
hereunto subscribed our names as witnesses thereto. We are of sound mind and proper age to witness
a will and understand this to be his/her will, and to the best of our knowledge testator is of legal age
to make a will, of sound mind, and under no constraint or undue influence.

_____ residing at _____

_____ residing at _____

Last Will and Testament

I, _____ a resident of _____ County, New York do hereby make, publish, and declare this to be my Last Will and Testament, hereby revoking any and all Wills and Codicils heretofore made by me.

FIRST: I direct that all my just debts and funeral expenses be paid out of my estate as soon after my death as is practicable.

SECOND: I give, devise, and bequeath the following specific gifts:

_____

_____

_____

THIRD: I give, devise, and bequeath the rest, residue and remainder of my estate, real, personal, and mixed, of whatever kind and wherever situated, of which I may die seized or possessed, or in which I may have any interest or over which I may have any power of appointment or testamentary disposition, to the following: _____

_____

_____

_____, or to the survivor of them.

FOURTH: In the event that any beneficiary fails to survive me by thirty days, then this will shall take effect as if that person had predeceased me.

FIFTH: I hereby nominate, constitute, and appoint _____ as Executor/Executrix of this, my Last Will and Testament. In the event that such named person is unable or unwilling to serve at any time or for any reason, then I nominate, constitute, and appoint _____ as Executor/Executrix in the place and stead of the person first named herein. It is my will and I direct that my Executor/Executrix shall not be required to furnish a bond for the faithful performance of his or her duties in any jurisdiction, any provision of law to the contrary notwithstanding, and I give my Executor/Executrix full power to administer my estate, including the power to settle claims, to borrow, pay debts, and sell, lease or exchange real and personal property without court order.

IN WITNESS WHEREOF, I declare this to be my Last Will and Testament and execute it willingly as my free and voluntary act for the purposes expressed herein and I am of legal age and sound mind and make this under no constraint or undue influence, this _____ day of _____, _____ at _____ State of _____.

_____L.S.

The foregoing instrument was on said date subscribed at the end thereof by
_____, the above named Testator who signed, published, and declared this instrument to be his/her Last Will and Testament in the presence of us and each of us, who thereupon at his/her request, in his/her presence, and in the presence of each other, have hereunto subscribed our names as witnesses thereto. We are of sound mind and proper age to witness a will and understand this to be his/her will, and to the best of our knowledge testator is of legal age to make a will, of sound mind, and under no constraint or undue influence.

_____ residing at _____

_____ residing at _____

Last Will and Testament

I, _____ a resident of _____ County, New York do hereby make, publish, and declare this to be my Last Will and Testament, hereby revoking any and all Wills and Codicils heretofore made by me.

FIRST: I direct that all my just debts and funeral expenses be paid out of my estate as soon after my death as is practicable.

SECOND: I give, devise, and bequeath the following specific gifts:

_____

_____

_____

THIRD: I give, devise, and bequeath the rest, residue and remainder of my estate, real, personal, and mixed, of whatever kind and wherever situated, of which I may die seized or possessed, or in which I may have any interest or over which I may have any power of appointment or testamentary disposition, to the following _____

_____

_____

_____, in equal shares, or their lineal descendants per stirpes.

FOURTH: In the event that any beneficiary fails to survive me by thirty days, then this will shall take effect as if that person had predeceased me.

FIFTH: I hereby nominate, constitute, and appoint _____ _____ as Executor/Executrix of this, my Last Will and Testament. In the event that such named person is unable or unwilling to serve at any time or for any reason, then I nominate, constitute, and appoint _____ as Executor/Executrix in the place and stead of the person first named herein. It is my will and I direct that my Executor/Executrix shall not be required to furnish a bond for the faithful performance of his or her duties in any jurisdiction, any provision of law to the contrary notwithstanding, and I give my Executor/Executrix full power to administer my estate, including the power to settle claims, to borrow, pay debts, and sell, lease or exchange real and personal property without court order.

IN WITNESS WHEREOF, I declare this to be my Last Will and Testament and execute it willingly as my free and voluntary act for the purposes expressed herein and I am of legal age and sound mind and make this under no constraint or undue influence, this _____ day of _____, _____ at _____ State of _____.

_____L.S.

The foregoing instrument was on said date subscribed at the end thereof by
_____, the above named Testator who signed, published, and declared this instrument to be his/her Last Will and Testament in the presence of us and each of us, who thereupon at his/her request, in his/her presence, and in the presence of each other, have hereunto subscribed our names as witnesses thereto. We are of sound mind and proper age to witness a will and understand this to be his/her will, and to the best of our knowledge testator is of legal age to make a will, of sound mind, and under no constraint or undue influence.

_____ residing at _____

_____ residing at _____

Codicil to the Will of

_____

I, _____, a resident of _____ County, New York declare this to be the first codicil to my Last Will and Testament dated _____, _____.

FIRST: I hereby revoke the clause of my Will which reads as follows:

_____

_____

_____

_____

SECOND: I hereby add the following clause to my Will: _____

_____

_____

_____

THIRD: In all other respects I hereby confirm and republish my Last Will and Testament dated _____, _____.

IN WITNESS WHEREOF, I have signed, published, and declared the foregoing instrument as and for a codicil to my Last Will and Testament, this _____ day of _____, _____.

_____

The foregoing instrument was on the _____day of _____, _____, signed at the end thereof, and at the same time published and declared by _____, as and for a codicil to his/her Last Will and Testament, dated _____, _____, in the presence of each of us, who, this attestation clause having been read to us, did at the request of the said testator/testatrix, in his/her presence and in the presence of each other signed our names as witnesses thereto.

_____ residing at _____

_____ residing at _____

This page intentionally left blank.

Self-Proved Codicil Affidavit

(attach to Codicil)

STATE OF NEW YORK

COUNTY OF _____

Each of the undersigned, individually and severally being duly sworn deposes and says:

The within codicil was subscribed in our presence and sight at the end thereof by _____, the within named testat_____, on the _____ day of _____, _____, at _____o'clock.

Said testat____ at the time of making such subscription declared the instrument so subscribed to be h____ last codicil to h___ last will.

Each of the undersigned thereupon signed h____ name as a witness at the end of said codicil at the request of said testat____ and in h___ presence and sight and in the presence and sight of each other.

Said testat____ was, at the time of so executing said will (codicil), over the age of 18 years and, in the respective opinions of the undersigned, of sound mind, memory and understanding and not under any restraint or in any respect incompetent to make a codicil.

The testat____, in the respective opinions of the undersigned, could read, write and converse in the English language and was suffering from no defect of sight, hearing or speech, or from any other physical or mental impairment which would affect h___ capacity to make a valid codicil. The codicil was executed as a single, original instrument and was not executed in counterparts.

Each of the undersigned was acquainted with said testat____ at such time and makes this affidavit at h___ request.

The within codicil was shown to the undersigned at the time this affidavit was made, and was examined by each of them as to the signature of said testat____ and of the undersigned.

_____(Witness)

_____(Witness)

Subscribed, sworn and acknowledged before me by _____, the testator, and by _____ and _____, witnesses, this _____ day of _____.

_____

Notary or other officer

This page intentionally left blank.

UNIFORM DONOR CARD

The undersigned hereby makes this anatomical gift, if medically acceptable, to take effect on death. The words and marks below indicate my desires:

I give:

(a) ____ any needed organs or parts;

(b) ____ only the following organs or parts

_____

for the purpose of transplantation, therapy, medical research, or education;

(c) ____ my body for anatomical study if needed.

Limitations or special wishes, if any:

_____

Signed by the donor and the following witnesses in the presence of each other:

_____	_____
Signature of Donor	Date of birth
_____	_____
Date signed	City & State
_____	_____
Witness	Witness
_____	_____
Address	Address

UNIFORM DONOR CARD

The undersigned hereby makes this anatomical gift, if medically acceptable, to take effect on death. The words and marks below indicate my desires:

I give:

(a) ____ any needed organs or parts;

(b) ____ only the following organs or parts

_____

for the purpose of transplantation, therapy, medical research, or education;

(c) ____ my body for anatomical study if needed.

Limitations or special wishes, if any:

_____

Signed by the donor and the following witnesses in the presence of each other:

_____	_____
Signature of Donor	Date of birth
_____	_____
Date signed	City & State
_____	_____
Witness	Witness
_____	_____
Address	Address

UNIFORM DONOR CARD

The undersigned hereby makes this anatomical gift, if medically acceptable, to take effect on death. The words and marks below indicate my desires:

I give:

(a) ____ any needed organs or parts;

(b) ____ only the following organs or parts

_____

for the purpose of transplantation, therapy, medical research, or education;

(c) ____ my body for anatomical study if needed.

Limitations or special wishes, if any:

_____

Signed by the donor and the following witnesses in the presence of each other:

_____	_____
Signature of Donor	Date of birth
_____	_____
Date signed	City & State
_____	_____
Witness	Witness
_____	_____
Address	Address

UNIFORM DONOR CARD

The undersigned hereby makes this anatomical gift, if medically acceptable, to take effect on death. The words and marks below indicate my desires:

I give:

(a) ____ any needed organs or parts;

(b) ____ only the following organs or parts

_____

for the purpose of transplantation, therapy, medical research, or education;

(c) ____ my body for anatomical study if needed.

Limitations or special wishes, if any:

_____

Signed by the donor and the following witnesses in the presence of each other:

_____	_____
Signature of Donor	Date of birth
_____	_____
Date signed	City & State
_____	_____
Witness	Witness
_____	_____
Address	Address

One of these cards should be cut out and carried in your wallet or purse.

INDEX

SPHINX® PUBLISHING ORDER FORM

BILL TO:		SHIP TO:	
Phone #	Terms	F.O.B. Chicago, IL	Ship Date

Charge my: ☐ VISA   ☐ MasterCard   ☐ American Express

☐ **Money Order or Personal Check**

Credit Card Number

Expiration Date

Qty	ISBN	Title	Retail	Ext.
		SPHINX PUBLISHING NATIONAL TITLES		
____	1-57248-363-6	101 Complaint Letters That Get Results	$18.95	____
____	1-57248-361-X	The 529 College Savings Plan (2E)	$18.95	____
____	1-57248-349-0	The Antique and Art Collector's Legal Guide	$24.95	____
____	1-57248-347-4	Attorney Responsibilities & Client Rights	$19.95	____
____	1-57248-148-X	Cómo Hacer su Propio Testamento	$16.95	____
____	1-57248-226-5	Cómo Restablecer su propio Crédito y Renegociar sus Deudas	$21.95	____
____	1-57248-147-1	Cómo Solicitar su Propio Divorcio	$24.95	____
____	1-57248-166-8	The Complete Book of Corporate Forms	$24.95	____
____	1-57248-353-9	The Complete Kit to Sellng Your Own Home	$18.95	____
____	1-57248-229-X	The Complete Legal Guide to Senior Care	$21.95	____
____	1-57248-391-1	The Complete Partnership Book	$24.95	____
____	1-57248-201-X	The Complete Patent Book	$26.95	____
____	1-57248-369-5	Credit Smart	$18.95	____
____	1-57248-163-3	Crime Victim's Guide to Justice (2E)	$21.95	____
____	1-57248-367-9	Employees' Rights	$18.95	____
____	1-57248-365-2	Employer's Rights	$24.95	____
____	1-57248-251-6	The Entrepreneur's Internet Handbook	$21.95	____
____	1-57248-235-4	The Entrepreneur's Legal Guide	$26.95	____
____	1-57248-346-6	Essential Guide to Real Estate Contracts (2E)	$18.95	____
____	1-57248-160-9	Essential Guide to Real Estate Leases	$18.95	____
____	1-57248-254-0	Family Limited Partnership	$26.95	____
____	1-57248-331-8	Gay & Lesbian Rights	$26.95	____
____	1-57248-139-0	Grandparents' Rights (3E)	$24.95	____
____	1-57248-188-9	Guía de Inmigración a Estados Unidos (3E)	$24.95	____
____	1-57248-187-0	Guía de Justicia para Víctimas del Crimen	$21.95	____
____	1-57248-253-2	Guía Esencial para los Contratos de Arrendamiento de Bienes Raices	$22.95	____
____	1-57248-103-X	Help Your Lawyer Win Your Case (2E)	$14.95	____
____	1-57248-334-2	Homeowner's Rights	$21.95	____
____	1-57248-164-1	How to Buy a Condominium or Townhome (2E)	$19.95	____
____	1-57248-328-8	How to Buy Your First Home	$18.95	____
____	1-57248-191-9	How to File Your Own Bankruptcy (5E)	$21.95	____
____	1-57248-343-1	How to File Your Own Divorce (5E)	$26.95	____
____	1-57248-222-2	How to Form a Limited Liability Company (2E)	$24.95	____
____	1-57248-231-1	How to Form a Nonprofit Corporation (2E)	$24.95	____
____	1-57248-345-8	How to Form Your Own Corporation (4E)	$26.95	____
____	1-57248-232-X	How to Make Your Own Simple Will (3E)	$18.95	____
____	1-57248-200-1	How to Register Your Own Copyright (4E)	$24.95	____
____	1-57248-104-8	How to Register Your Own Trademark (3E)	$21.95	____
____	1-57248-233-8	How to Write Your Own Living Will (3E)	$18.95	____
____	1-57248-156-0	How to Write Your Own Premarital Agreement (3E)	$24.95	____
____	1-57248-230-3	Incorporate in Delaware from Any State	$26.95	____
____	1-57248-158-7	Incorporate in Nevada from Any State	$24.95	____
____	1-57248-250-8	Inmigración a los EE.UU. Paso a Paso	$22.95	____
____	1-57071-333-2	Jurors' Rights (2E)	$12.95	____
____	1-57248-223-0	Legal Research Made Easy (3E)	$21.95	____

Qty	ISBN	Title	Retail	Ext.
____	1-57248-165-X	Living Trusts and Other Ways to Avoid Probate (3E)	$24.95	____
____	1-57248-186-2	Manual de Beneficios para el Seguro Social	$18.95	____
____	1-57248-220-6	Mastering the MBE	$16.95	____
____	1-57248-167-6	Most Val. Business Legal Forms You'll Ever Need (3E)	$21.95	____
____	1-57248-360-1	Most Val. Personal Legal Forms You'll Ever Need (2E)	$26.95	____
____	1-57248-098-X	The Nanny and Domestic Help Legal Kit	$22.95	____
____	1-57248-089-0	Neighbor v. Neighbor (2E)	$16.95	____
____	1-57248-388-1	The Power of Attorney Handbook (5E)	$22.95	____
____	1-57248-332-6	Profit from Intellectual Property	$28.95	____
____	1-57248-329-6	Protect Your Patent	$24.95	____
____	1-57248-385-7	Quick Cash	$14.95	____
____	1-57248-344-X	Repair Your Own Credit and Deal with Debt (2E)	$18.95	____
____	1-57248-350-4	El Seguro Social Preguntas y Respuestas	$14.95	____
____	1-57248-217-6	Sexual Harassment: Your Guide to Legal Action	$18.95	____
____	1-57248-219-2	The Small Business Owner's Guide to Bankruptcy	$21.95	____
____	1-57248-168-4	The Social Security Benefits Handbook (3E)	$18.95	____
____	1-57248-216-8	Social Security Q&A	$12.95	____
____	1-57248-221-4	Teen RIghts	$22.95	____
____	1-57248-366-0	Tax Smarts for Small Business	$21.95	____
____	1-57248-335-0	Traveler's Rights	$21.95	____
____	1-57248-236-2	Unmarried Parents' Rights (2E)	$19.95	____
____	1-57248-362-8	U.S. Immigration and Citizenship Q&A	$16.95	____
____	1-57248-387-3	U.S. Immigration Step by Step (2E)	$24.95	____
____	1-57248-392-X	U.S.A. Immigration Guide (5E)	$26.95	____
____	1-57248-192-7	The Visitation Handbook	$18.95	____
____	1-57248-225-7	Win Your Unemployment Compensation Claim (2E)	$21.95	____
____	1-57248-330-X	The Wills, Estate Planning and Trusts Legal Kit	&26.95	____
____	1-57248-138-2	Winning Your Personal Injury Claim (2E)	$24.95	____
____	1-57248-333-4	Working with Your Homeowners Association	$19.95	____
____	1-57248-380-6	Your Right to Child Custody, Visitation and Support (3E)	$24.95	____
____	1-57248-157-9	Your Rights When You Owe Too Much	$16.95	____
		CALIFORNIA TITLES		
____	1-57248-150-1	CA Power of Attorney Handbook (2E)	$18.95	____
____	1-57248-337-7	How to File for Divorce in CA (4E)	$26.95	____
____	1-57248-145-5	How to Probate and Settle an Estate in CA	$26.95	____
____	1-57248-336-9	How to Start a Business in CA (2E)	$21.95	____
____	1-57248-194-3	How to Win in Small Claims Court in CA (2E)	$18.95	____
____	1-57248-246-X	Make Your Own CA Will	$18.95	____
____	1-57248-196-X	The Landlord's Legal Guide in CA	$24.95	____
____	1-57248-241-9	Tenants' Rights in CA	$21.95	____
____		**Form Continued on Following Page**	**SubTotal**	____

To order, call Sourcebooks at 1-800-432-7444 or FAX (630) 961-2168 (Bookstores, libraries, wholesalers—please call for discount)

Prices are subject to change without notice.

Find more legal information at: **www.SphinxLegal.com**

SPHINX [barcode] FORM

Qty	ISBN	Title	Retail	Ext.

FLORIDA TITLES

Qty	ISBN	Title	Retail	Ext.
___	1-57071-363-4	Florida Power of Attorney Handbook (2E)	$16.95	___
___	1-57248-396-2	How to File for Divorce in FL (8E)	$28.95	___
___	1-57248-356-3	How to Form a Corporation in FL (6E)	$24.95	___
___	1-57248-203-6	How to Form a Limited Liability Co. in FL (2E)	$24.95	___
___	1-57071-401-0	How to Form a Partnership in FL	$22.95	___
___	1-57248-113-7	How to Make a FL Will (6E)	$16.95	___
___	1-57248-088-2	How to Modify Your FL Divorce Judgment (4E)	$24.95	___
___	1-57248-354-7	How to Probate and Settle an Estate in FL (5E)	$26.95	___
___	1-57248-339-3	How to Start a Business in FL (7E)	$21.95	___
___	1-57248-204-4	How to Win in Small Claims Court in FL (7E)	$18.95	___
___	1-57248-381-4	Land Trusts in Florida (7E)	$29.95	___
___	1-57248-338-5	Landlords' Rights and Duties in FL (9E)	$22.95	___

GEORGIA TITLES

Qty	ISBN	Title	Retail	Ext.
___	1-57248-340-7	How to File for Divorce in GA (5E)	$21.95	___
___	1-57248-180-3	How to Make a GA Will (4E)	$21.95	___
___	1-57248-341-5	How to Start a Business in Georgia (3E)	$21.95	___

ILLINOIS TITLES

Qty	ISBN	Title	Retail	Ext.
___	1-57248-244-3	Child Custody, Visitation, and Support in IL	$24.95	___
___	1-57248-206-0	How to File for Divorce in IL (3E)	$24.95	___
___	1-57248-170-6	How to Make an IL Will (3E)	$16.95	___
___	1-57248-247-8	How to Start a Business in IL (3E)	$21.95	___
___	1-57248-252-4	The Landlord's Legal Guide in IL	$24.95	___

MARYLAND, VIRGINIA AND THE DISTRICT OF COLUMBIA

Qty	ISBN	Title	Retail	Ext.
___	1-57248-240-0	How to File for Divorce in MD, VA and DC	$28.95	___
___	1-57248-359-8	How to Start a Business in MD, VA or DC	$21.95	___

MASSACHUSETTS TITLES

Qty	ISBN	Title	Retail	Ext.
___	1-57248-128-5	How to File for Divorce in MA (3E)	$24.95	___
___	1-57248-115-3	How to Form a Corporation in MA	$24.95	___
___	1-57248-108-0	How to Make a MA Will (2E)	$16.95	___
___	1-57248-248-6	How to Start a Business in MA (3E)	$21.95	___
___	1-57248-209-5	The Landlord's Legal Guide in MA	$24.95	___

MICHIGAN TITLES

Qty	ISBN	Title	Retail	Ext.
___	1-57248-215-X	How to File for Divorce in MI (3E)	$24.95	___
___	1-57248-182-X	How to Make a MI Will (3E)	$16.95	___
___	1-57248-183-8	How to Start a Business in MI (3E)	$18.95	___

MINNESOTA TITLES

Qty	ISBN	Title	Retail	Ext.
___	1-57248-142-0	How to File for Divorce in MN	$21.95	___
___	1-57248-179-X	How to Form a Corporation in MN	$24.95	___
___	1-57248-178-1	How to Make a MN Will (2E)	$16.95	___

NEW JERSEY TITLES

Qty	ISBN	Title	Retail	Ext.
___	1-57248-239-7	How to File for Divorce in NJ	$24.95	___

NEW YORK TITLES

Qty	ISBN	Title	Retail	Ext.
___	1-57248-193-5	Child Custody, Visitation and Support in NY	$26.95	___
___	1-57248-351-2	File for Divorce in NY	$26.95	___
___	1-57248-249-4	How to Form a Corporation in NY (2E)	$24.95	___
___	1-57248-401-2	How to Make a NY Will (3E)	$16.95	___
___	1-57248-199-4	How to Start a Business in NY (2E)	$18.95	___
___	1-57248-198-6	How to Win in Small Claims Court in NY (2E)	$18.95	___
___	1-57248-197-8	Landlords' Legal Guide in NY	$24.95	___
___	1-57071-188-7	New York Power of Attorney Handbook	$19.95	___
___	1-57248-122-6	Tenants' Rights in NY	$21.95	___

NORTH CAROLINA TITLES

Qty	ISBN	Title	Retail	Ext.
___	1-57248-185-4	How to File for Divorce in NC (3E)	$22.95	___
___	1-57248-129-3	How to Make a NC Will (3E)	$16.95	___
___	1-57248-184-6	How to Start a Business in NC (3E)	$18.95	___
___	1-57248-091-2	Landlords' Rights & Duties in NC	$21.95	___

NORTH CAROLINA AND SOUTH CAROLINA TITLES

Qty	ISBN	Title	Retail	Ext.
___	1-57248-371-7	How to Start a Business in NC or SC	$24.95	___

OHIO TITLES

Qty	ISBN	Title	Retail	Ext.
___	1-57248-190-0	How to File for Divorce in OH (2E)	$24.95	___
___	1-57248-174-9	How to Form a Corporation in OH	$24.95	___
___	1-57248-173-0	How to Make an OH Will	$16.95	___

PENNSYLVANIA TITLES

Qty	ISBN	Title	Retail	Ext.
___	1-57248-242-7	Child Custody, Visitation and Support in PA	$26.95	___
___	1-57248-211-7	How to File for Divorce in PA (3E)	$26.95	___
___	1-57248-358-X	How to Form a Croporation in PA	$24.95	___
___	1-57248-094-7	How to Make a PA Will (2E)	$16.95	___
___	1-57248-357-1	How to Start a Business in PA (3E)	$21.95	___
___	1-57248-245-1	The Landlord's Legal Guide in PA	$24.95	___

TEXAS TITLES

Qty	ISBN	Title	Retail	Ext.
___	1-57248-171-4	Child Custody, Visitation, and Support in TX	$22.95	___
___	1-57248-399-7	How to File for Divorce in TX (4E)	$24.95	___
___	1-57248-114-5	How to Form a Corporation in TX (2E)	$24.95	___
___	1-57248-255-9	How to Make a TX Will (3E)	$16.95	___
___	1-57248-214-1	How to Probate and Settle an Estate in TX (3E)	$26.95	___
___	1-57248-228-1	How to Start a Business in TX (3E)	$18.95	___
___	1-57248-111-0	How to Win in Small Claims Court in TX (2E)	$16.95	___
___	1-57248-355-5	The Landlord's Legal Guide in TX	$24.95	___

SubTotal This page _____

SubTotal previous page _____

Shipping— $5.00 for 1st book, $1.00 each additional _____

Illinois residents add 6.75% sales tax _____

Connecticut residents add 6.00% sales tax _____

Total_ _____

To order, call Sourcebooks at 1-800-432-7444 or FAX (630) 961-2168 (Bookstores, libraries, wholesalers—please call for discount)

Prices are subject to change without notice.

Find more legal information at: **www.SphinxLegal.com**